▼ *The Packing Book* ▼

The Packing Book

Secrets of the Carry-on Traveler

· 3rd Edition ·

Judith Gilford

Ten Speed Press
Berkeley, California

In loving memory of my father, Morton Elkins

1➲

TEN SPEED PRESS
P.O. Box 7123
Berkeley, CA 94707
www.tenspeed.com

Distributed in Australia by Simon and Schuster Australia, in Canada by Ten Speed Press Canada, in New Zealand by Southern Publishers Group, in South Africa by Real Books, in Southeast Asia by Berkeley Books, and in the United Kingdom and Europe by Airlift Book Company.

Cover design by Nancy Austin

Text design by Victor Ichioka

Cover and text illustrations by Richard Sigberman

Library of Congress Cataloging-in-Publication Data
Gilford, Judith.
    The packing book: secrets of the carry-on traveler /
Judith Gilford. — Rev. ed.
      p. cm.
Includes bibliographical references.
ISBN 1-58008-021-9
   1. Travel I. Title
G151.G54 1996
910'.2'02—dc20   96-10864
              CIP

First printing this edition 1998
Printed in Canada
3 4 5 6 7 — 04 03 02 01 00

CONTENTS

▼ Acknowledgments

Many thanks to the following knowledgeable people and organizations for contributing interviews and materials:

Pamela Bracken, Overseas Adventure Travel (OAT); Bill Dawson, REI Adventure Tours; and David Kalter, Hostelling International/ American Youth Hostels (AYH), for sharing the outstanding packing lists that are used in their adventure travel programs; wardrobe consultants Carol Bell, Joyce Beadle, Linda Curyea, Karen Snow, and Laura Santi; Kevin Reid, Keeble and Schuchat Photography; Keith Taylor, REI; Dick Ellenwood and A. W. Kershaw, The Walk Shop; Susan Lee, Tutto Luggage; Buck Tilton, Wilderness Institute; Robin Pinné, Sierra Designs; Patty Gafvert and Tracy Tallar, Ex Officio; Chris Gubera, Adventure Medical Kits; Skip Kotkins, Jr., LLGMA; Joe Carrol, T.W. Carrol & Co. and International Luggage Repair Association (ILRA); Chris Patel, Stuffed SHIRT Co.; Alan Petit; Aris Export; Elliot Wahba and staff, Norm Thompson; Don Rosberg, Norma Beckstead, and Gloria Bertiglia, Westwind; Christopher Dennis, Edwards Luggage; Larry Kruger, Coconuts; Jeff Brady and Steve Pfeiffer, Camp 7, MEI; Jeffrey Longbrake, Flexo-Line; Cathryn Hartnett, L. L. Bean; Barbara Starner, Remin Kart-a-Bag; Ruth Nichols, Samsonite; Mike Harrelson, Patagonia; Debbie Licolli and Barry Gevertz, Lullaby Lane; Nancy Gold, Tough Traveler; Sally DeMasi, Wolf Computer; Hank Verbais, FAA Office of Public Affairs; Dee Donaldson, Accent on You; Suzanne Hogsett, Mrs. Milton Valois, William Wotkyns, Tarponwear, Railriders.

Thanks also to all my family members and friends for their moral support, ideas, information, and babysitting; and especially to Kathleen Keough, Roger Rapoport, Peter Beren, Kai Wessels, George Young, Kirsty Melville, Aaron Wehner, Heather Garnos, Nancy Austin, Rich Sigberman, Leili Eghbal, Cynthia Traina, Lisa Ryers, Lauren Webb, Victor Ichioka, Christa Laib, Frances Bowles, Sharilyn Hovind, Bruce Lobree, Julie Lavezzo, Michael Marcuson, Laura Sheppard, Sharon Todd, and the entire staff of Easy Going.

My continued special thanks to my husband, David, for his love, logic, and unwavering faith; to Nathan and Sara, for their cheerful hugs, patience, and understanding (and help with the kids' section); and especially to my incredible mother, Thelma Elkins, founder of Easy Going, who has been telling me for years that "it oughtta be a book!"; and especially in memory of my wonderful father, Mort Elkins, for his encouragement, optimism, and humor.

Introduction: Singing the Overpacker's Blues

Welcome to Overpackers Anonymous! If you've ever experienced that sinking feeling while staring at your bed on the night before departure, clothes piled high and an open suitcase on the floor, this is the book for you. Perhaps you suffer from the "just-in-case" syndrome, convinced you have to take every piece of clothing you own on a two-week trip. Do you feel compelled to pack a different fashion garment for morning, noon, and night?

We all know the consequences—being weighed down by luggage, dependent on others for help, waiting in endless lines, and constantly managing "inventory." And for what? Most people don't use half of what they bring and swear that the next time will be different.

Don't worry—you're not alone. In my years of teaching packing seminars at Easy Going Travel Shop and Bookstore in Berkeley, California, and for large corporations, clothing stores, and civic organizations, I have discovered that everyone—even the most seasoned traveler—worries about packing. I do, too! The overwhelming interest in *The Packing Book* has further proven that "packing anxiety" strikes a chord in every traveler. For good reason. You're leaving home for an unfamiliar destination, without the security of your familiar possessions. What if you underpack and leave home without some essential you need? What if you can't find what you need when you get there? "What if?" is the question that plagues us all.

Another problem is that every trip is different. You've just mastered packing for formal business trips, but then you decide to tack on a beach vacation, or the family decides to go for a weekend getaway. Sometimes you go by air, sometimes by car, or perhaps by train. Sometimes you don't care how much your bag weighs, while at other times traveling light is crucial in order to negotiate the trip. *The Packing Book* will be useful no matter what kind of trip you are taking *this time*.

"This time" can mean a formal five-day business trip, a family weekend getaway, a week at a beach resort, or a three-week combination work and play vacation in two climates.

Finding balance is the key. Whether you go carry-on or decide to check your bag, you really can pack everything you need in order to feel comfortable on the road with a single manageable suitcase plus an optional secondary bag.

This book is designed to make you feel more confident about packing efficiently so that you can enjoy your full measure of mobility and independence on the road. I'll discuss what luggage to buy, what clothes to wear and how to maintain them on the road, what travel accessories you will need, and how to organize yourself in general. And I'll also show you a great packing technique.

With modern innovations in luggage, clothing fabrications, and portable travel gear, we travelers are fortunate to live in an age when traveling light has never been easier.

So have no fear, overpackers, you'll soon be on the road to recovery!

▼ Your Traveling Lifestyle and a Flexible Packing Plan

Trips vary in the activities they entail, how mobile you want to be, and the level of choice that you want in your wardrobe and accessories. Some trips require more formal clothing, while others are entirely casual. Sometimes you want to be self-sufficient and travel very light. At other times you want to have a bigger wardrobe and more accessories, even if the trade-off is heavier luggage. Sometimes you want as much variety as possible and will accept heavier luggage and perhaps even two pieces. But don't worry, because by using this book, you'll be able to get there carry-on, whatever your traveling lifestyle! For those of you who plan to check your luggage, you'll still learn to travel lighter by using this book.

Remember, planning is the essential key to anxiety-free packing. Even if you aren't leaving next week, read the background information, so that when you're ready to hit the road, you will have put together a versatile wardrobe that you can pack in less time than you would have believed possible.

1

The Carry-on Craze

Let's play travel trivia. Here are three questions for you:

1. How many pieces of luggage are handled by the airlines each year?
2. How many pieces of luggage are lost by the airlines each year?
3. What happens to all that lost luggage?

Now, the answers. The airlines handle more than 700 million pieces of luggage annually. They lose approximately one percent. This isn't bad. But where does all that lost luggage end up? In Alabama, according to the *San Jose Mercury News* (December 10, 1989). Apparently, once the airlines have made every effort to find the owners and have failed to do so, the bags and their contents are sold, in wholesale lots, to merchants in Scottsboro, Alabama. Here, the merchandise is displayed in small storefronts and sold, retail, at discount prices.

And that's not all; there's more bad news. According to a recent report in the *Los Angeles Times*, luggage theft by employees is on the rise. In two FBI operations, Grab Bag and Ramp Check, at O'Hare International Airport in Chicago, agents "seized $250,000 worth of goods and cash and filed charges against sixteen airport workers, accusing them of taking jewelry, video equipment, mink coats, cash, and even guns from passengers' bags." The article went on to say that the thieves in Chicago allegedly concentrated on baggage being transferred from one airline to another, because responsibility was difficult to assign. The U.S. attorney in Chicago said that the thieves simply "zipped or ripped bags open, took what they liked, then sent the luggage on its way, some of it 'pretty well torn up.' Stolen goods were often stashed in public areas until the end of the rogue baggage handler's shift. By one account, an airport security guard knowingly helped carry booty to the thief's car." This type of internal theft at major airports is being reported around the country, in addition to the usual thefts from passengers who fail to keep an eye on their luggage in waiting areas. What's more, nearly all airline carriers exclude valuables most likely to be stolen—camera equipment, jewelry, computers, and cash—from liability coverage.

▼ Why Go Carry-on?

Obviously, the fear of losing their luggage or belongings is the main reason that many travelers these days want to carry it on the plane. Also, it's faster: carrying your own luggage allows you to bypass the carousels at the airport and move right on to your destination. Business people are especially taken with carry-on, as they want to get off the plane and get right to their appointments (time is money). Some travelers prefer to be self-sufficient, especially when they are touring many destinations that are off the beaten track. Diverse modes of transportation often create the need to be able to manage luggage without help from porters.

There are times, however, when carry-on luggage is neither necessary nor practical—if you plan to check in your luggage on a nonstop flight; if you require bulky cold-weather clothing or gear; if your health prevents you from handling your own luggage; if your luggage is being handled for you by the tour company; if you are going on a formal business trip and need several suits or dresses; if you are traveling with small children and lots of equipment; if you are going on a cruise that requires several outfits, evening gowns, tuxedos, and so on; or, if you are in the fashion business and *must* have ten pairs of shoes and sixteen outfits, all unrelated. For the rest of us, my carry-on strategy will simplify life on the road.

This book focuses on carry-on travel because more and more travelers are discovering that carry-on is not only desirable, but also feasible on all kinds of trips. The designs and fabrics of carry-on luggage have become very sophisticated. Leisure and business clothing is available in a variety of fabrics that are relatively wrinkle-resistant. Travel accessories and weather gear are available to provide comfort and protection without enormous bulk. And, as I'll show you, there is an effective technique for packing all of these items in a carry-on.

If you want to carry on your luggage, you will need to reorient your packing mentality. Carry-ons are a big change from the 29-inch suitcase you may be used to checking in. The reduced space means that you have to make choices about living on the road. Once you have chosen a traveling lifestyle, you will be able to choose a suitable wardrobe and accessories. This book will *teach* you to travel light.

▼ Carry-on Guidelines

The determination to carry on all their luggage has driven passengers to board with anything and everything imaginable, from computers to giant toys to shopping bags full of pineapples. This might be convenient for the owners, but it wreaks havoc on the other passengers trying to board and on the safety standards promoted by the flight attendants. It is not uncommon for heavy items to rain down from overhead bins during turbulence, injuring passengers and crew. Airline unions have been agitating for stricter regulation and enforcement regarding the number of bags and sizes of carry-on luggage.

The Federal Aviation Administration states only that bags that are brought aboard must fit under the seat or in the overhead bin. Each airline is free to define its own limits on the number, size, and weight of carry-on luggage, and it is up to the gate attendants to be as lenient or as strict as they care to be.

Their decision is influenced by the size of the aircraft (commuters have less space than jumbo jets), whether the plane is full, half-full, or empty, and whether it is a long international flight. They may be more lenient toward passengers traveling in first and business class.

Size

Generally the upper limit for carry-on luggage to be stowed *under the seat* is 45 inches overall. When you add up the length, height, and depth of the bag (measured in inches), the sum should be no more than 45 inches. This includes suitcases measuring between 20 and 22 inches long—that is, 20 × 16 × 9 inches, or 21 × 16 × 8 inches, or 22 × 14 × 9 inches (the maximum size). The 21- and 22-inch models are best for packing wardrobes.

The 8- or 9- inches-deep measurement is the crucial one here. Anything more than 10 inches deep will be hard to stuff overhead or under the seat. Keep in mind that softsided luggage will expand when packed, so don't overstuff it, or you'll have trouble stowing it. For safety reasons and the health of your back muscles, plan to pack so that you can stow your heavier bag under the seat rather than overhead.

Carry-on sizes vary according to the type of airplane you are flying in. Some airlines will allow only 39 inches under the seat, room enough for a small totebag (about 17 inches long). Foreign-based airlines (which also tend to be more strict), international flights, commuter airlines, and airlines using smaller aircraft are more likely to have lower limits. Keep in mind that different aircraft used by the same airline will have different-sized compartments. It is best to call ahead *to each airline you plan to fly* and ask about its carry-on regulations. Get the information sent or faxed to you, so that you can carry it with you to avoid arbitrary decisions by airline staff. On some aircraft, aisle seats tend to have a bit less luggage space, so, if you have a full-sized under-seat bag, ask for a window or middle seat.

The upper limit for the overhead compartment on many airlines is 60 inches overall. This will accommodate larger, wider items such as folded garment bags, which may measure 22 × 8 × 23 inches. However, on many aircraft, the compartment is much smaller. *Keep the length of your suitcase or garment bag (folded in half) to about 22 inches to be on the safe side.* Longer items will be dealt with on a case-by-case basis. For safety's sake, try to keep the overhead compartment for larger, more stable suitcases, or light smaller ones. Luggage carts should be placed under your seat.

Number

Most airlines allow you one or two pieces of carry-on luggage. You are also allowed to check through one or two other items, for a *total* of three or four pieces of luggage. So, if you are planning to check additional luggage through, make sure to find out from each airline you plan to fly on what your *total* luggage allotment is, with any weight limitations, and how much of it may be carried on.

Counted as carry-on pieces are garment bags, suitcases, briefcases, travelpacks, daypacks, totebags, camera cases, computers and computer cases, shopping bags, and duty-free bags. Note: You are allowed *up to* a total circumference of 45 inches for underseat luggage, so two small bags that will fit underneath together count as one.

About Garment Bags

Garment bags have their place as carry-on luggage. The general size limitation is 72 inches, or 45 × 4 × 23 inches (open). They are useful if you are on a business trip or vacation where you'll need multiple suits or formal dresses. If not stuffed too full, they can be brought aboard and stowed in a closet or, folded in half, in the overhead bin. Many people like being able to hang everything up all at once at the hotel.

However, garment bags have limitations. First, most aircraft have little or no closet space in which to stow these heavy "mobile homes." If you don't get there first, the closet will be full and you will have to stow the bag overhead or check it. Second, meeting the closet's 8-inch-deep limitation will be impossible if the garment bag is packed with the usual requirement for a two- or three-week trip. Folded over, the bag may be too fat to fit overhead, so you will have to check it. Garment bags are also unwieldy to lug if you are taking public transportation on your own, although some models, such as Samsonite's Silhouette 5, feature wheels and a retractable handle.

For those reasons, garment bags are not my first choice. Much more useful is a 21-inch or 22-inch carry-on suitcase in the form of a shoulder bag, convertible pack, or wheeled bag, with a suiter option to accommodate a suit or jacket.

Additional Carry-on Items

As well as one or two carry-on bags, most airlines allow you to take on board with you other miscellaneous items. These generally, but not always, include a handbag, overcoat or wrap, umbrella, binoculars, camera (35 mm, without carrying case), a reasonable quantity of reading material, prosthetic devices (canes, braces, crutches), and unopened liquor, which, if you want to drink, must be served to you by the flight attendant. Travelers with infants are usually allowed an infant-necessities bag, a blanket, a small stroller that can fit overhead, and/or possibly a car seat, if there is room on the plane. Luggage carts may or may not be counted.

Prohibited Items

The following hazardous items, *among others*, are prohibited in carry-on or checked luggage: flammables, mace, tear gas and other eye irritants, propane, butane cylinders or refills, cigarette lighter refills, any equipment containing fuel, safety or "strike-anywhere" matches, solvents, and aerosols. There are certain exceptions for personal care, medical needs, sporting equipment, and items to support physically challenged travelers. For example, flammable toiletries and medicinal articles such as perfume, matches, and lighters may be carried on your person. Pocket knives with blades over 4 inches long are also prohibited unless they are checked. Call your airline regarding any specific items you are concerned about.

Using Portable Electronic Devices on the Plane

Federal regulations prohibit airline passengers from using portable telephones or two-way radios on board. Many other devices can be taken on board but their use is prohibited while the plane is taxiing, taking off, and landing. Each airline has the right to impose its own regulations, and flight crews can impose stricter ones if necessary. Here are some examples. Call your airline to verify pertinent information.

Items generally allowed — Portable voice recorders, electric shavers, calculators, laptop computers with attached mice, accessory printers and tape drives, handheld electronic games without remote controls, typewriters, CD players (sometimes not allowed), electronic toys without remote controls, video camcorders (sometimes not allowed), video players, tape cassette players, beepers, audio tape players, and pagers.

Items generally not allowed — Radios, AM and FM transmitters and receivers, televisions, portable cellular telephones, electronic games, toys and computers with remote controls, cordless computer mice, and CB radios and other transmitting devices. (From *San Jose Mercury News*, July 4, 1993.)

▼ More Isn't Better— The *Real* Carry-on Allotment

Having just read the list of all the things that airlines allow you, you overpackers are probably thinking right now, "Great! I can take *everything* with me."

A gentle reminder: Carry-on is not about lugging all your worldly possessions with you wherever you go. Carry-on is about mobility, about freedom, about traveling *light*. The focus of this book is on planning, selecting, and taking *only what you need*.

Our definition of *carry-on* will be *one* manageable carry-on bag that will fit underneath the seat or in the overhead bin on the airplane, and in storage facilities when you are traveling around. For added convenience or a measure of luxury, you may also want to bring a second, smaller bag such as a tote or daypack. If you prefer to check your luggage, limit yourself to a 24-inch bag. You can still use the information here to travel lighter.

▼ Carry-on Courtesy and Boarding Tips

Don't let carry-on travelers get a bad rap from their fellow passengers, who routinely complain about their transgressions. Follow these tips— especially if flights are over 60% full.

1. Board the flight early. You will have more time to find your seat and a space for your luggage without bumping into other passengers.

2. Take only the number and size of bags allowed by each airline you plan to fly.

3. The overhead bins are for the belongings of two to three people. Do not take more than your own space. Don't use your space and then go hunting five or ten rows back for additional storage.

4. When boarding and disembarking, handle your bags carefully so you don't bump people in front of or behind you. Be patient.

5. The bulk of in-flight injuries are caused by luggage tumbling down from the overhead bins at the end of a flight. To avoid injuring passengers and crew:

a) tuck away or remove garment bag hooks. These catch on other bags and cause everthing to tumble down.

b) choose fabric over smooth leather business cases. These slide out easily and fall on other passengers.

6. Pack lightly enough that you can lift your main bag into the overhead compartment yourself, without having to rely on an attendant to help you. Place heavier items in your smaller bag and store it under your seat. Luggage carts go underseat as well.

7. If you have a rigid-frame bag, such as a wheelaboard, plan on putting it overhead unless it is 20 inches long. It is very hard to maneuver rigid bags into the underseat compartment.

8. Aisle seats tend to have a bit less luggage space, so, if you have a full-size underseat bag, ask for a window or middle seat. Emergency exit rows have better legroom and easier access to underseat spaces, too.

9. Always be prepared to (graciously) check your luggage if the attendant deems it necessary. Label your luggage inside and out, lock your bags, and keep your hotel itinerary in an outside pocket, in case your luggage arrives after you do.

2

Smart Luggage

Choosing the right luggage is crucial to traveling light. The wrong bag can defeat you if it is too heavy, uncomfortable to carry, cheaply made, the wrong size, the wrong style, or not weatherproof. The right piece of luggage can help you be an organized, self-sufficient traveler, will be a dream to pack, and will be easy to manage. There are three types of luggage suitable for carry-on travel: the 45-inch carry-on (21 or 22 inches in length), the hanging garment bag, and the totebag or daypack. If you are determined to go carry-on and travel freely, limit yourself to the 45-inch bag as your main bag. Properly packed, it can handle almost any kind of wardrobe. If mobility is not essential, or you have a larger, bulkier wardrobe, consider the garment bag. You can make use of plastic dry cleaning bags, and the garment bag provides a convenient hanging closet when you reach your destination. If you intend to check your luggage or simply want more room, a 24-inch suitcase is your best bet.

Garment bags are great for extended business trips as well as for cruises that require a lot of formal wear, but they do have their limitations. They are not reliable carry-ons. Airplane closets fill up quickly. As a result you may have to fold your bag into an overhead compartment. If the bag is packed lightly, it will fit overhead; but, if packed fully and folded in half, it could be too large for the overhead compartment and will then have to be checked. Garment bags are also unwieldy to carry about while sightseeing and may be difficult to stow in lockers or on public transportation.

▼ Coordinating a Luggage System

When buying luggage, don't just think of individual pieces. Think of selecting a system, a configuration that enables you to be as mobile and hands-free as possible. You will be traveling with a main bag and a secondary, smaller bag. When choosing your pieces, think of how they all work together for comfort when boarding and disembarking, walking long distances, and loading and unloading. Don't overload your shoulders. Always try to have one hand free to open doors, make phone calls, or write a note.

▼ Your Main Bag: Choosing a 45-inch Carry-on

Your largest bag will hold the bulk of your clothing and some or all of your gear. Useful 45-inch carry-on styles (21 or 22 inches in length) include the shoulder bag, the travel pack (convertible backpack), and the wheeled bag. To be able to pack as described in this book (see chapter 5), choose a bag with a three-sided zipper that makes it possible to open it flat like a book.

In choosing a bag, consider:

- ▼ How you want to carry it (on your shoulders, on your back, or by its own wheels)
- ▼ How much you will be carrying it (take into account types of transportation and activities)
- ▼ Terrain and handling conditions (rough? normal? rugged?)
- ▼ How you want to organize and pack it
- ▼ Your long-term traveling needs

Shoulder Bags

Shoulder bags are suitcases with a handle and a detachable shoulder strap. Semisoft versions have a structured frame created by piping and foam padding that hold the bag's shape during packing. Their main attraction is ease of organization: they come in one-, two-, and three-compartment designs. They also compress easily to fit into tight spaces. Quality brands include the Easy Going Special Edition Bag, Lark, Tumi, Hartmann, Boyt, Andiamo, Samsonite, Land's End, L. L. Bean,

REI, Patagonia, Caribou, Eagle Creek, and Tough Traveler. If you are carrying a fully loaded shoulder bag, I recommend taking a luggage cart as well.

A three-compartment, 45-inch carry-on shoulder bag.

THREE-COMPARTMENT SHOULDER BAGS

A three-compartment bag, such as the 21-inch Easy Going Special Edition, is the perfect high-capacity, all-purpose bag for short trips, extended trips, or trips requiring two wardrobes. Make sure that at least two of the compartments where you will pack clothing open completely. You can stow warm-weather casual clothing in one section, business or cold weather wear in the second, and use the third compartment for your gear. These bags are packing-friendly because each compartment is supported by piping and foam padding and keeps its shape during packing. Wardrobes fit snugly, so they wrinkle less. The Easy Going bag has easy-to-grasp, lockable zipper pulls, comfortable handle and shoulder straps, and a "top-load" outer compartment that prevents small accessory items from falling out. I use an Easy Going Special Edition Bag for business or leisure, for weekend, week-long, and longer trips. For weekends I have shared it with my husband and kids!

TWO-COMPARTMENT SHOULDER BAGS

Two-section bags are useful for short trips and simple wardrobes. They allow the traveler to separate clothing from accessories or the washed from the unwashed. Additional outside pockets help organize accessories.

A one-compartment pullman,
packed with the bottom layer of accessories.

ONE-COMPARTMENT SHOULDER BAGS

People like one-compartment pullman-type bags because they are so easy to pack and a single zipper provides access to all their belongings. Some bags come with a movable partition that converts them into a two-compartment bag. Wheels, a selling point for many travelers, are available only on one-compartment bags. Some, such as Tutto's carry-on pullman, come with four wheels and a pullbar. Others, like the Travelpro Rollaboard, come with two built-in wheels and a telescoping handle.

A travel pack (convertible backpack)
with detachable daypack.

Travel Packs (Convertible Backpacks)

The travel pack, sometimes called a convertible backpack, has become popular because it is versatile and easily carried. Designed by backpacking companies, they are incredibly sturdy and many can stand up to rough travel and handling conditions. These are suitcases that transform themselves. When carried horizontally, they are single cavity shoulder bags. When turned vertically, the bags can be converted to backpacks: a hip belt and shoulder straps are stowed in the back panel. If you are doing a lot of sightseeing or walking or need to run for connections, it is a real blessing to be able to transfer 80 percent of the weight of your luggage off of your shoulders onto your hips. Many travel packs come with extra features such as side pockets and a detachable daypack (which can act as your second piece of luggage). Keep in mind that, to meet carry-on regulations, such accessories must be emptied or detached for the flight.

Travelers planning to carry on their luggage must choose a convertible pack according to size (the main compartment must be no more than 9 × 14 × 22 inches) rather than fit. Many travel packs come in larger sizes. Unfortunately, they are too large to carry on. Manufacturers of good quality travel packs include Camp 7, MEI, Eagle Creek, REI, Patagonia, L. L. Bean, JanSport, Caribou, and Tough Traveler.

There are two types of packs suitable for general travel:

FRAMELESS TRAVEL PACKS

"Convenience level" travel packs come with padded shoulder straps and a padded waistband, but have no other substantial means of support, such as an internal frame. You can carry this model on your back or sling one strap over your shoulder for that last dash at the airport. These packs are suitable for light packers and kids, when loads do not exceed 20 pounds. They are lighter and less expensive than packs with internal frames.

INTERNAL-FRAME TRAVEL PACKS

The "intermediate level" internal frame travel packs make it easy to carry heavier loads. Designed to adjust to your torso length, these bags are mounted on hidden aluminum stays that give the pack stability. A foam or plastic sheet offers back support and comfort from poking items. Typically these packs feature adjustable shoulder, hip and sternum straps and a lumbar pad. Extras include a zip-off day pack, outside pockets, and in the case of the Camp 7 line, a "stuff-it flap/organizer pocket" that allows you to stow a jacket on the outside of the pack while providing handy access to necessities. They may also have lash straps so that you can attach a sleeping bag or other gear. Some travel packs, such as the Camp 7 De Leon or the Eagle Creek Switchback, feature a telescoping handle and wheels, so it acts like a wheelaboard. The Switchback has a panel that folds down to cover the wheels and provide padding against the body when it is used as a pack, but no waistband. The Camp 7 wheelaboard pack offers a padded hipbelt.

"Advanced level" travel packs offer features that you would look for on more technical packs, such as still beefier waistbands, shoulder straps, and the like. Indeed, these packs can be used for backpacking as well as general travel, which may fit your long term plans. Prioritize fit over size if you need this kind of pack.

Internal-frame packs have three advantages: They are versatile, easily carried, and comfortable. If you want to buy only one bag for year-round use as conventional luggage and for outdoor activities such as hiking or backpacking, buy this style. It will give you the maximum freedom for sightseeing, hiking, and touring around with your luggage in tow. The attached daypack on models such as those made by Camp 7 makes it a self-contained unit when you are traveling. Internal-frame packs can be fitted to your body, providing the most comfort for a wide range of activities. All packs differ in fit. Buy the one that fits you the best and still meets carry-on regulations. If your torso is long and fit is important for the activities you plan, you may have to choose a larger size and forgo the convenience of carrying it on the aircraft.

Wheeled Bags

Wheeling one's luggage seems to be irresistible. But, before you select wheeled luggage or a luggage cart, assess your needs. If you need one carry-on, a wheeled suitcase or a lightweight luggage cart may be the answer to your prayers. But if you are a constant traveler who carries large loads, if you tend to load the cart with extras, or if you have a family, you may need a heavy-duty luggage cart. Extra weight on wheeled suitcases or lightweight carts can cause the handle to bend or even break. Remember that the more hardware there is, the more there is to break! Also, some airlines insist on checking wheeled bags and/or will not be responsible for damage to them. If this concerns you, choose another option.

WHEELED LUGGAGE

The hottest trend in luggage is bags that feature a rigid frame, telescoping handle, and built-in wheels. Because of their frames, these bags won't let you overpack! On all models, it is possible to attach a second tote, briefcase, or even a folded garment bag on top of the built-in bag, so that you travel unencumbered.

There are wheeled models designed to appeal to every traveler's needs. Wheelaboards come in all shapes and sizes, from 20-inch underseaters to large 29-inch suitcases. Remember that maximum carry-on size is 22 inches. 24-inch and 26-inch bags are typical check-through sizes.

Most models are vertically oriented, with two wheels. Some models, such as Tutto, feature four sturdy wheels riveted on a nearly indestructible external frame. The bag's weight rests on the ground, not against your body. A U-shaped pull bar is anchored to the outer

Tutto's 24-inch pull-along.

edges of the frame. This provides extra stability for fingertip control and easy 360° maneuverability. The Tutto bag can be loaded on top with other bags, or even sat upon! People with arthritis or back problems will find these models particularly helpful. For this reason, Tutto was the winner of the Arthritis Foundation Design Award, as well as being top-rated for durability by *Consumer Reports* (May 1994).

All wheeled models are one-compartment pullmans. Some, such as the Travelpro Crew Plus series, offer separately a handy plastic insert that divides the inner space in half, creating a shelf on which you can place your clothing. (If yours doesn't have one, make your own out of light cardboard, or check with Travelpro or a Travelpro dealer.)

There are various kinds of wheelaboards. "Suiter" models allow you to hang a jacket, suit, or dress inside. This is an important innovation and a real boon for business and leisure travelers. Atlantic features a suiter model with a see-through compartment to store folded shirts in the lid as well. Other models function as portable offices, with convenient outside pockets that hold your computer, office supplies, and files. You can sit at the airport and work right out of your suitcase, keeping your hands free of a separate briefcase or computer bag. Eagle Creek and Camp 7 make wheelaboards that double as travel packs (see Resources p. 193).

Wheelaboards are perfect for concourses, airports, and conventional urban travel. If you will be on rough terrain or in outlying areas, a travel pack, wheeled travel pack, or shoulder bag with a heavy-duty luggage cart may be more appropriate. Also keep in mind that although it has wheels, there will be times when you need to hoist it up overhead in a plane or bus—so watch the weight, both when you buy it and as you pack.

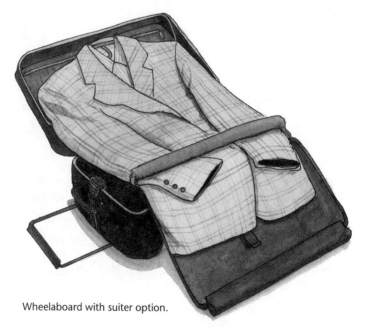

Wheelaboard with suiter option.

When shopping, check for a strong frame, good finish work, coil zippers that go around three sides of the bag, and sturdy rubber or urethane rollers, or in-line–skate wheels tthat are inset in the bag. For maximum packability, select thin walls and as much unobstructed inner space as possible. You want the full $19^1/_2$ to $21^1/_2$ inches for packing! For stability, I prefer wheels on the wide, rather than narrow, side of the bag. The telescoping handles should be easy to open and close (do you need one hand or two?) and should lock in the open and closed positions. There are many types of handles and they are not interchangeable—make sure you can quickly and easily acquire replacement parts for servicing if needed. Two grab handles, one at the top and one at the side, are handy for easy lifting. Also pick the configuration of outside pockets that suits you. Gusseted pockets are more easily accessed and hold more than flat slash pockets. Collapsibility can also be handy. Tutto luggage collapses to $3^1/_2$ inches for under-the-bed storage—no more waiting in long lines to retrieve your luggage at the end of a cruise!

There are many, many brands of wheelaboards in all price ranges. Andiamo, Atlantic, Briggs and Reilly, Boyt, Delsey, Eagle Creek and Camp 7 (convertible backpacks-cum-wheelaboards), Hartmann, Kiva, Lark, Samsonite, Travelpro, Traveler's Choice, Tumi, and Tutto are all quality brands.

Vertical wheelaboard with telescoping handle.

▼ Choosing a Garment Bag

A garment bag can act as your main bag. There are numerous garment bags on the market, in all price ranges. As with all luggage, choose the one that fits your needs. Consider first the length of your trips, as well as the clothing you will need. Garment bags are suitable for suits, dresses, evening gowns, tuxedos, and hanging dress shirts. Hanging bags come in 2- to 4-suit depths, and may be 42, 48, 52, or 56 inches long. If you choose a longer version, look for a bag that will fold into thirds so as to fit under the seat or overhead. A simple garment cover will protect that one tuxedo or wear-it-once formal outfit, or suffice for an overnight trip. Some bags come with wheels.

A semisoft garment bag is piped to keep its structure. Make sure the outside hook is detachable or stowable so it does not dangle. A bar at the top supports the weight the bag is designed for. Do not over-pack or the bar may bend. Access to the hangers is important, too. Convenient models have a self-supported swing-out curtain. The curtain opens like a door, allowing full access to the interior. A handy hook keeps the curtain out of the way as you pack.

Look for a lightweight, weather- and stain-resistant fabric, such as cordura or ballistic nylon. The hanger system (such as the Wally Lock) should allow use of regular wire hangers and prevent clothes from falling off. Make sure the handle is comfortable. Zipper openings should be oriented correctly whether the bag is in the folded or extended position. Many bags have pockets for accessories, shoes, and soiled clothing; look for an organizational setup you like. Tie straps inside are handy.

Note: Make sure that the top outside hanger clip can be removed or stowed easily. These dangling hardware pieces often get caught on other items in the overhead bins during flight and are a major cause of passenger injuries when they cause other items to tumble down at the end of a flight.

▼ Your Second Bag: Choosing a Totebag or Daypack

It is convenient to have access to items you need on the plane and during the day without having to return to your main bag. Daypacks, shoulder totes, and duffels can hold the day's money in a small wallet, medicine, glasses, water bottle, a sweater, quick change of clothes, guidebook, map, writing materials, tissues, lip balm, sunscreen, makeup, a small camera, and so on. Business travelers will want something for a cell phone, computer and computer equipment, files and business materials, as well as personal items. (See also Camera, Computer, and Business Bags on the following page.)

For the plane, in case your main bag is checked, consider stocking your hand luggage with an extra shirt, set of underwear, and toiletries, so that you will not be entirely inconvenienced if the bag is lost. *Your second bag should be lockable.*

The "Last Minute" Bag

In addition to or instead of your second bag, take along a sturdy foldup zippered nylon bag that expands to become a suitcase. It is indispensable to every traveler. This "Last Minute Bag" offers the luxury of being stowable, so you don't have to carry a second bag until you need to take it out. Unfolded, it acts as anything from a totebag to a shopping bag or laundry bag once you reach your destination. You can also use it to bring home souvenirs and other extras. Easy Going sells a wonderful 20-inch, carry-on–size expandable suitcase that has a lockable zipper. It is strong enough to handle trade show catalogs and heavy items. Other options in this category include French-style string bags and fanny packs that fold out to become daypacks, made by Eagle Creek.

DAYPACKS

The daypack is the most versatile second bag for the casual traveler. A daypack can be worn on the back or shoulders, leaving your hands free. You can use it on day hikes, stowing your suitcase in a locker or hotel room. Choose a daypack made of lightweight parachute nylon, pack-cloth, or cordura nylon. Many travel packs conveniently come with a detachable daypack as part of the unit, which is invaluable when boarding and disembarking.

Select a model with at least one pocket on the outside, padded shoulder straps, and a handle at the top. Double zippers allow easy access when the bag is stowed. Attach a combination lock and you have a fairly safe place for your camera.

SHOULDER TOTES

A lightweight shoulder tote is good for general touring. If you will be out all day and into the evening without returning to your hotel, you will want a tote big enough to hold a quick change of clothing, shoes, or accessories, plus your umbrella, raincoat, guidebook, and camera. There are a variety of styles by all major manufacturers. Choose one that coordinates in function with your main bag. Your shoulder tote should lock. The Last Minute Bag can also act as a tote.

FANNY PACKS

Fanny packs are great for traveling, especially if you do not carry a second bag. For extra security, thread the waistband through your belt loops. Do not use a fanny pack for valuables such as passport, money, tickets, credit cards, and so on. *Those should be carried only in a security wallet.* (See chapters 3 and 10.)

▼ Camera, Computer, and Business Bags

Camera bags, briefcases, and laptop computer bags are considered to be carry-on luggage. Therefore, you need a multifunctional bag that will hold your camera or computer equipment as well as other business and personal items. These bags come in every configuration imaginable, made by almost all of the major luggage, photography, and outdoor companies. Pick a case that is high quality, comfortable to wear, and easy to work from. For security reasons, I prefer inconspicuous styles and a locking case.

Note: Smooth-sided briefcases are a major cause of in-flight injuries. They fall out when the overhead bins are opened. For safety reasons, consider a fabric bag instead of leather.

Aside from standard briefcases, travelers can choose a casual looking but sturdy padded briefcase shoulder bag with adjustable inserts for computer equipment. Look for these in outdoor, photography, luggage, and travel stores. I like models that have a place for a water bottle on the outside. Also, some wheelaboard lines, such as Travelpro, offer computer and camera cases that attach to your wheelaboard. Tutto makes a very fine "Office-on-Wheels," a 20 × 13 × 8-inch case with an external frame and four wheels that is pulled by a U-shaped pullbar. I like it because it is top loading for easy access and can carry heavy loads easily (so you don't have to). It's particularly good when you have samples, binders, catalogs, paper, computer equipment, and the like, and excellent for people with back problems or arthritis. Tough Traveler makes the Gembac, a computer bag that can be worn as a shoulder bag or backpack.

Photographers may also want a shoulder bag, and quality versions are made by Tenba, Tamrac, Lowepro, Domke, Photoflex, Sun Dog, Ruff-Pack, and Billingham. Many of these double as computer bags. Some are full-sized, while others have body-hugging, thin-profile designs. Tenba makes camera bags specifically for laptop computers, and the Ventures line includes the neat little Detachable Film Net Pocket, a nylon mesh see-through film pouch with a handle. It fits into the top of the shoulder bag and is easily detached for hand inspection at the airport X-ray machine. (For tips on carrying film, see pp. 55–56.)

Active photographers and adventure travelers prefer fanny packs or modular bags because they allow maximum mobility and leave the hands free. In Photoflex's Galen Rowell line, the main camera bag (either the medium capacity Modular Waist Pack or the larger Modular Shoulder Bag) can be worn around the waist on a specially designed padded waist belt. Small accessory cases can be added. The waist belt also accommodates the Rowell backpack for clothing. The Photoflex bag has a lid that opens away from you so that you can use both hands for the equipment. Movable dividers enable you to reconfigure the bag to make room for everything from a long lens to a video recorder.

Lowepro's Orion Trekker, a fanny-pack–style camera bag, includes a separate snap-on daypack for clothing, food, and necessities. When not needed, the daypack folds neatly into the front pocket of the bag.

Those with a lot of equipment should consider camera backpacks: full-sized bags with adjustable backpack straps and hip belts. Lowepro makes the Photo Trekker in a carry-on size (13 × 6 × 19 inches). Tamrac makes the Super Photo Backpack (12 × 6 × 21 inches) and the smaller Summit Photo Backpack (12 × 6 × 18 inches).

Video tapes, computer disks, and credit cards can all be ruined by the magnetic field found in inspection equipment at the airport. Put these items through the conveyor belt and not the metal detector.

Look for these features when shopping for camera and computer bags:

▼ The outer shell materials should provide protection against impact, abrasion, tearing, and the weather. Ballistic nylon or cordura nylon should be 1,000-denier or more, with a weather-resistant urethane coating. The two fabrics are equally strong, but ballistic nylon is less abrasive and looks more elegant than cordura does. Cordura is more abrasion- and slash-resistant. Canvas is not as waterproof or as rugged as synthetics are, but it is lighter, less expensive, less abrasive, and conforms more readily to body shape. Domke and Billingham make fine canvas bags.

▼ Make sure that the inner padding is made of closed-cell foam or other lightweight composite padding, not open-cell foam, which will flatten or degrade over time.

▼ Look for versatile padded insert walls with movable partitions.

▼ Make sure that the buckles, rings, and zippers are of high quality, easy to use, and resistant to cold weather.

▼ Make sure the pockets have storm flaps for protection in wet weather.

▼ A rigid floor prevents the sides from caving in when the bag is lifted.

▼ General Luggage-Buying Guidelines

When buying new luggage, the old adage, "you get what you pay for" really is true. There are all types of luggage in all price catagories, and they may look surprisingly similar. But performance is almost always related to price. Luggage differs in its ability to withstand the demands of travel and modern day baggage handling systems. Its performance depends upon the quality of the fabric, frame, zipper, handle, and hardware that is used, and its general workmanship. Keep in mind that what seems expensive in the short run will save you money and inconvenience in the long run.

Define what it is that you expect from your luggage, and buy accordingly. The LLGMA (Luggage and Leather Goods Manufacturers of America) recommends that you purchase luggage to meet your most demanding traveling needs. People who travel extensively for business or for "adventure," or who often check through their luggage, have different luggage needs than those who enjoy occasional leisurely travel. Your luggage retailer can help you make the best purchase if s/he knows what your needs and expectations are.

Read the luggage warranty carefully. Know what types of damage the manufacturer does and does not cover. Try to choose a retailer and manufacturer that will service your luggage quickly and inexpensively in case it needs repair. If your bag is damaged by the airline, the airline will most likely be responsible for the claim.

For security reasons, I prefer inconspicuous styles that do not draw attention. Copy or cut out the luggage checklist at the end of this chapter and take it with you to the store when you shop for luggage. All luggage should lock.

When shopping, look for the following construction features to determine quality and prevent the likelihood of damage:

FABRIC

For maximum durability, select 1000 denier cordura or 2500 denier ballistic nylon. These fabrics are sturdy enough to withstand abrasion and tearing with sharp objects. Moderate use luggage may be made of 500 denier or 1800 denier polyester, a cordura look-alike; these are not quite as tear or abrasion resistant, but suffice when durability is not a priority issue. They are less expensive than cordura or ballistic nylon, and for many travelers, do the trick. 600 denier polyester doesn't hold up very well, and vinyl tends to crack or tear over time and should be avoided.

Other features that protect fabric from abrasion are plastic curb slides, found on the lower backside of the suitcase, and corner protectors. These add years of life to a bag.

WEATHERPROOFING

Look for polyurethane coating (PUC) of at least 1 or $1^{1}/_{4}$ ounces on the fabric to prevent moisture from drowning the bag. Other fabrics may have other treatments. Dye should not bleed when wet. Some bags have a Teflon coating on the outside for stain and soil resistance.

HANDLE

Look for comfortable carry handles, either a loop and flap design (two straplike handles joined with a small patch of leather) or single handle (like that on a standard suitcase). The handles should be riveted securely to the bag with strong hardware.

Retractable "telehandles" on rolling suitcases should be easy to open and close with one hand and lock into place in both the down and the up position. Locking in the down position can prevent damage resulting from the handle pulling out and being hit by something on the conveyor belt in the baggage handling system. Locking in the up position can mean that you can push or pull the bag without the handle succumbing to pressure. Some bags may have a two-position lock to adjust to the user's height. Some luggage features recessed wells for the telehandle and zippered covers to protect the handle if checked through. Check for handle durability and ask your retailer or manufacturer if the parts are readily available.

FRAME/WHEEL ASSEMBLY

On wheeled luggage, the frame and retractable handle and wheel assembly can be external or internal. An external assembly will, by necessity, result in the suitcase itself being a bit smaller, in order to allow the overall dimensions to conform to carry-on size guidelines. Internally-placed handles will give you added packing space, even though the bottom of the suitcase will not be flat (it will house the handle). You must weigh your decision based your priorities—i.e., how much you can get into the bag vs. other features that may be important to you. The frame, wheels, and handle assembly should be of the highest quality you can afford.

WHEELS

Wheels should be of rubber urethane, or inline skate-wheel material. If they are detachable, remove them if you intend to check the bag. Make sure the hardware is securely fixed. On roll-aboard bags, look for recessed wheels. The one exception is Tutto luggage, which has non-recessed wheels that have been rated number one in *Consumer Research* for durability.

SHOULDER STRAP

The shoulder strap should be wide, adjustable, and removable. Look for good hardware and a nonslip shoulder pad for comfort. Padded replacement shoulder straps are available in specialty travel stores and outdoor equipment stores.

ZIPPERS

For maximum durability choose #10 nylon coil zippers. These are sturdy, work smoothly and will not fail if a tooth breaks. Metal zippers have a greater tendency to jam or snag clothing; plastic is less sturdy than nylon. Choose zippers with two pull tabs that come together and close with a little combination or key lock. On semi-soft bags, double zippers allow easy access even if the bag is stowed beneath the seat in front of you.

STITCHING

Look for double stitching. Finished seams cost more money but will not fray.

FLOOR

The floor distributes the weight of the bag's contents and prevents sagging when the bag is lifted. Bags with structured floors are easier to pack. The floor also determines the way the bag is stored. Most semi-soft bags have a padded cardboard or plastic insert to lend structure but allow the bag to be compressed when not in use. Rigid-framed bags have two types of floors. A rigid folding floor means that the floor is attached on only one side. When pressed into place, the bag has a rigid floor; when flipped up, the bag compresses for compact storage. A fixed floor means that the bag cannot be compressed when stored. Soft luggage has no floor reinforcement.

COLOR

Generally, light colors show dirt the most; dark colors tend to show the effects of abrasion fairly quickly.

▼ Luggage Carts

A luggage cart is a collapsible carrier that is ideal for pushing or pulling your luggage along concourses, streets, and even up and down stairs. They are indispensable to many travelers, are generally accepted aboard the aircraft *in addition* to carry-on luggage, and are easily stowed. I strongly recommend a luggage cart if you are taking a shoulder bag.

Carts can accommodate two or more pieces of luggage, making them appropriate for couples or families. You can use a luggage cart with your existing bag if you do not want to buy wheeled luggage. Used with a shoulder bag, they make luggage effortless to tow, adding immeasurably to your mobility. The best ones are easily collapsed and set up and come with sturdy wheels, a stepslider, and a wide platform for added stability.

Assess your long-term needs and your travel lifestyle in choosing a luggage cart. If you travel light, buy a durable, high-quality lightweight cart, such as Remin's FliteLite C525. For long-term multipurpose use, when you are taking heavier loads over various types of surfaces, stairs, and curbs, invest in a heavy-duty cart, such as Remin's Concert III, which has large wheels, a wide platform, and stepslider.

Remin Kart-a-Bag makes special models for salespeople who carry computers or sample cases; trade show representatives who carry displays and materials; musicians; photographers; and numerous other mobile businesspeople. The company lends carts to its customers and offers a one-day turnaround on repairs.

Make sure you buy a durable luggage cart with unbreakable joints, heavy-duty telescoping tubing, and dependable wheels. It should have:

▼ Adequate carrying capacity—100 pounds is average for the smallest; some will carry up to 175 pounds

- The ability to remain upright when put down in a collapsed position
- A mechanism to lock it in place when upright so that luggage can be loaded and unloaded easily
- High-quality wheels, *at least* 3 inches in diameter (or 4 to 6 inches for added stability on staircases, curbs, or cobblestones)
- An adequately wide base for multiple bags and added stability
- A size when folded that enables it to fit under the seat or overhead for storage
- A reasonable weight—between $3\frac{1}{2}$ and 7 pounds (naturally the heavier carts are more durable)
- Permanently attached elastic cords on the base

Optional but highly desirable features include:

- Stair or curb slides
- A garment-bag attachment so that you can drape a dress or suit bag over your luggage

▼ Luggage Accessories

Here are some items you may need to purchase in addition to your luggage.

Identifier — A ribbon, tape, pom pom, or other unique identifier will distinguish your bag on the carousel if you check through.

Luggage tags — Tags can fall off, so label your luggage inside and out. For security reasons, use your name and business address and telephone number or your destination address and telephone number. In the event you check your bag, an itinerary placed in an outside pocket will help lost luggage reach you instead of being sent home.

Retractable luggage lock — This is a cable lock with a combination that allows you to fasten your luggage to a park bench or other stationary object and allows you to take your eyes off the luggage.

Luggage locks — All your luggage should lock. You can use small locks for double-zippered suitcases. I recommend the combination type that you set yourself, as there are no keys to lose.

Padded shoulder strap(s)

Pull strap(s)

Luggage straps — These are nylon webbing straps, 1, 1$\frac{1}{2}$, or 2 inches wide. They offer additional protection in transit. They are especially valuable for wheelaboards. Thread the strap lengthwise around the bag, *over* the closed retractable handle and *under* the grab handle, to minimize the chance of the bag being picked up by the wrong handle.

Luggage alarm — The alarm sounds if someone attempts to take your bag.

▼ Preventing Damage to Your Suitcases

USE COMMON SENSE WHEN CHECKING LUGGAGE

1. Only check luggage that is sturdy enough to withstand airline baggage handling systems.

2. Never check a bag that doesn't completely close. If you need a luggage strap or bungee cord to keep the bag closed, it probably won't survive the trip.

3. Never check a bag that has broken components, such as wheels, handles, zippers, latches and locks.

4. Never check a bag that is meant to be carried on. Most briefcases, tote bags, plastic garment covers, and items received through retail promotions are not designed to be checked luggage.

5. Don't overpack. Overpacking puts a strain on zippers, seams, frames and hinges.

6. Clearly label luggage with your name, current address, and phone number.

7. Check your bag carefully in the luggage claims area before departing the airport.

8. Consider replacing old or worn luggage. Luggage that is several years old may not be able to withstand today's automated baggage handling systems.

WHAT TO DO ABOUT DAMAGED LUGGAGE

Report any damage immediately to the baggage service center of the airline on which you traveled. Damage claims should be filed before leaving the airport. By not following this procedure, you risk that the damage will not be covered under warranty or airline policy. (See p. 189 for more on this topic.)

HAVE A COMPLAINT ABOUT DAMAGED LUGGAGE?

Write:
Aviation Consumer Protection Division
U.S. Department of Transportation C-75
400 7th St., SW, Room 4107
Washington, DC 20590

▼ Luggage Buyer's Checklist: 45-Inch Carry-on Bag

	Model 1	Model 2	Model 3	Model 4
Brand/name				
Store				
Price				
Weight				
Dimensions				
Volume				
Fabric				
Color				
Structured sides				
# compartments	1 2 3	1 2 3	1 2 3	1 2 3
Pockets, outside				
Pockets, inside				
Handle				
Shoulder strap				
Zippers				
Tie straps				
Storage				
Other features				
Travel packs				
Zip-off daypack				
Internal frame				
Frameless				
Other features				
Wheeled bags				
Wheels, recessed or protruding				
Curb skids				
Handle, back or side				
Grab handle, side and/or top				
Other features				

This checklist is useful in making comparisons among various items of luggage. When considering travel packs and wheeled bags, take the additional elements into consideration as well.

Reprinted courtesy of Luggage and Leather Goods Manufacturers of America.

3

Travel Gear

After choosing luggage, your next priority is putting your travel gear together: equipment and incidentals that you will need or want while away from home. Each item must be chosen carefully according to need, usefulness, weight, and size. Only pack essentials. Remember that there are many useful items, but if you take them all you will need three suitcases!

To cut down, find out what will be available at your destination. Share with a travel companion. Think of what you might find, improvise, or do without along the way. In choosing gear, think miniature. Scout backpacking stores, travel stores, and drug stores for compact and lightweight models.

When making your packing list, think first of the essentials—gear related to your safety, health, and hygiene—that will serve daily use. These are basics and generally do not change from trip to trip. Examples would be your toothbrush and cap, a travel alarm, a flashlight, a security wallet, sunscreen and hat, travel soap, a water bottle, a small sewing kit. For me, this also includes items that it would cause great inconvenience to be without in case of an emergency or at night when stores are closed, such as a pocketknife, eyeglass repair kit, a first aid kit including Alka Seltzer, Pepto Bismol, ibuprofen, Band-Aids, a nightlight.

Essentials also include any gear that is directly related to the climate and your activities, such as camera equipment for safari, binoculars for birdwatching or a cruise, insect repellent and mosquito netting for the tropics, or raingear and a travel umbrella for a European tour.

Next add items that you simply must have to make you a happy traveler. These vary from person to person, from true minimalists who figure they can "make do" or improvise along the way, to others who might feel that these items make the difference between a good trip and a great trip. These can be an inflatable pillow, a walkman with tapes, a book, a white noise machine, a small coffee maker, a hairdryer, a musical instrument. Keep in mind that it is you who will do the lugging, so try to be conservative here and cut down somewhere else.

Finally there is gear for the "self-sufficient traveler." This person might bring a spoon and hot/cold cup, a picnic kit, a towel, sleep sheets, a tool kit, office supplies, or film mailers. A woman alone might carry a hotel intruder alarm.

Use the following checklists to help organize your list and give you ideas. Then complete your list, and go back over it with a critical eye. Try to eliminate as much as possible.

At the end of your trip, look at your list again. Note items that you overpacked and items that you wished you had brought. Save the list for your next trip, and you'll be on your way to being a very efficient packer.

▼ The Bare Essentials Checklist

This list contains items that can become necessary on any trip and provide a minimum level of self-sufficiency. For expanded lists, read further on in this chapter. For basic lists, see Quicklists in the back of the book.

- ☐ security wallet
- ☐ travel alarm or watch with alarm
- ☐ toiletry kit: toothbrush w/cap, toothpaste, dental floss, deodorant, travel soap, moist towelettes, sunscreen, lip balm, moisturizer, shampoo and conditioner, razor/blades, tube of shaving cream, nail clipper, tissue pack, comb, folding brush, sanitary items, birth control, toilet seat covers, eyecare supplies
- ☐ medical kit : prescription medicines, antacid, diarrhea medicine, pain/fever reliever, muscle relaxer, cold pills

- [ ] first aid kit: antiseptic wipes, Band-Aids of all sizes, moleskin, tweezers, eyeglass repair kit, insect repellent, anti-itch cream
- [ ] clothing care kit: sewing kit, travel soap or detergent, clothesline, inflatable hanger, stain stick, strong clips, sink stopper
- [ ] pocketknife with scissors, tweezers, corkscrew, bottle/can opener
- [ ] flashlight with extra battery and bulb
- [ ] water bottle/snack/purifier if needed
- [ ] notebook and pen
- [ ] money exchange calculator
- [ ] small camera, film, and batteries
- [ ] hat/small umbrella/packable raincoat
- [ ] set of earplugs
- [ ] plastic bag for wet and soiled items
- [ ] foldup, nylon, expandable bag
- [ ] photographs of your family
- [ ] language phrasebook
- [ ] guidebook
- [ ] map, magnifier, compass, highlighter pen
- [ ] nightlight

Security Wallets

Your first consideration is your method of carrying valuables. I urge you to take some kind of security wallet to carry your passport, money, traveler's checks, credit cards, airline tickets, and an extra copy of your eyeglass and medication prescriptions. *Never put your valuables in a wallet, fanny pack, daypack, purse, carry-on, or checked luggage.* These are suitable for a bit of cash for the day, but not for the bulk of your resources. Valuables should go on your person, hidden underneath your clothes. Remember to select clothing that will accommodate the security wallet; assume that you will be wearing it all the time.

In selecting a security wallet, consider weather resistance, the type of clothing you will be wearing, and how you want to wear the wallet—around your neck or your waist, under your shoulder, around your leg, or, as a comfortable hanging wallet, tucked along your thigh like a pocket. I prefer adjustable styles such as the World Class Passport Carrier by Coconuts. I don't like neck pouches because the neck straps invite trouble. Materials should be weather-resistant. If you are going to tropical climates, choose a cotton- or Cambrelle-backed money pouch—it will be cooler than nylon is—or use one that hangs like a pocket.

WORLD CLASS PASSPORT CARRIER

This is a versatile wallet that can be worn with all styles of clothing. It can be used as a hanging loop wallet, a money belt around your waist, or as a shoulder holster. The loop has a steel cable running through it. The detachable, adjustable strap also has a steel cable inside so that it cannot easily be cut off. The nylon pouch has three sections: the front section has a pocket for an American passport and credit cards; the middle zippered section will hold cash and traveler's check (the money is thus invisible when you need to pull out only your passport at a checkpoint or bank); the rear compartment has room for tickets and other documents. Other nice features include a diagonal zipper, which prevents the contents from falling out, and a polyurethane coating for

The World Class Passport Carrier, with waistband.

weather-resistance. There are no external seams to fray or tear. There are two sizes available, allowing for variation in ticket quantity and size.

The most comfortable, coolest, and most accessible way to wear a security wallet is to fasten it to your belt or strap it around your waist and then tuck it down your skirt, slacks, or shorts. When you need something in it, pull it up and out, and tuck it back—it remains attached to you at all times.

AROUND-THE-WAIST SECURITY WALLETS

These standard money pouches will hold a passport, money, and tickets. I do not recommend them for hot weather (although when made of cotton they are less uncomfortable), but many people prefer them. Eagle Creek makes a nice line with a Cambrelle-fabric backing that is more absorbent than cotton is and dries much faster.

NECK POUCHES

The best way to wear a neck pouch is actually around your waist, tucked inside your skirt, shorts, or slacks. They are great for unbelted clothing, such as skirts and shorts, and are ideal for women. If you wear it around your neck, do not let the straps show. The Undercover Security Wallet made by Eagle Creek is my favorite because it has an adjustable strap and an outside zip pocket that makes it easy to retrieve a little cash or a credit card without taking the whole thing out.

SHOULDER HOLSTERS

Though they make access more difficult, shoulder holsters are generally favored by men. Do not forget to wear them under your shirt, not just under your jacket.

LEG POUCHES

These come in leather or elasticized nylon spandex and fit around the calf or ankle.

MONEY BELTS

The conventional-looking belts have a zippered compartment on the inside for storing folded cash. They come in woven fabric or leather.

WATERTIGHT POUCHES

The Seal Pack, useful for carrying your valuables at the beach, is a convenient, watertight security wallet that can be worn around your waist while you are swimming. Eagle Creek also makes a watertight pouch called the Salamander.

CLOTHING WITH POCKETS

Many specially designed travel clothes feature sewn in security pockets. A half-slip with concealed pockets is available from The Primary Layer catalog. Among other manufacterers, Norm Thompson makes Frequent Flyer Jackets with concealed pockets, too. (See Resources p. 197 for both.)

▼ Money and Travel Documents

These items should be stowed in your security wallet. Pack as applicable:

- ☐ passport/photo ID
- ☐ cash/foreign currency
- ☐ credit cards
- ☐ checks
- ☐ ATM card (two can be handy in case one demagnetizes)
- ☐ telephone card
- ☐ traveler's checks (half in your money belt, half in your daybag)
- ☐ airline, bus, and train tickets (photocopy tickets in case they get lost)
- ☐ driver's license or international driver's license
- ☐ auto club card
- ☐ A 3 × 5-inch card with emergency phone numbers (including main home contact, a 24-hour travel agent, medical and auto insurance, U.S. embassies and consulates, and doctors at your destination). See Appendix 4 for details.
- ☐ copies of medical and eyeglass or contact lens prescriptions
- ☐ medical history/list of allergies, etc.
- ☐ list of addresses

- [ ] student I.D. card or hostel pass
- [ ] train pass or voucher
- [ ] visa(s); extra passport photos
- [ ] other _____
- [ ] other _____

Pack the following in an accessible wallet or, better yet, a brightly colored, flat zippered nylon organizer pouch about 5 × 7 inches in size:

- [ ] cash and tip money—enough for the day only
- [ ] coins
- [ ] receipts, ticket stubs, and other "collectibles"

Other Documents

In your suitcase, store an envelope with photocopies of important documents and any other papers and photographs you might want. Keep the other half of your traveler's checks and half of your prescription medications here, too. Choose yet a third place for your traveler's checks record and list of any PIN and calling-card access codes you need to remember.

For maximum safety, copies of all this information should also be with a home contact person. Keep their phone number in your security wallet. In case of theft, you can call your contact to cancel your cards and send you anything you need.

- [ ] copy of passport (all pages)
- [ ] copies of medical and eyeglass or contact lens prescriptions
- [ ] vouchers and confirmations
- [ ] phone number of ground transportation provider
- [ ] other half of your traveler's checks
- [ ] PIN and phone-card access codes
- [ ] international telephone and cell phone dialing instructions
- [ ] traveler's checks record
- [ ] medical, auto, and travel insurance papers
- [ ] itinerary/copies of airline tickets
- [ ] frequent flyer cards, vouchers, and numbers

- [ ] sales receipts for any equipment to be declared at customs
- [ ] customs declaration papers
- [ ] immunization certificate
- [ ] health forms/allergies/medical history/special medications
- [ ] list of gifts and sizes
- [ ] other _____
- [ ] other _____

▼ Organizing Your Travel Gear

Make little kits to organize your personal items. For example, assemble all your toiletries in one kit, and make up others for medical needs, laundry, first aid, office supplies, bedside needs, picnicing, etc. Small kits allow the most flexibility in using packing space, compared to bulky hanging organizers and dopp kits. They are also easy to transport out of the bag to the location where they will be used in your room. Clear or brightly colored pouches in different colors provides color-coding, which makes kits easy to find and their contents known. Always choose the smallest pouch or organizer that will hold what you need. You can use plastic bags in various sizes (the quart and gallon sizes are handiest), colored nylon pouches, or any type of lightweight, slim organizer or toiletry kit. Hanging models are handy for outdoor use or when sharing facilities. I prefer water-repellent, colorful, zippered nylon pouches such as those made by Club USA and Outdoor Research. Adventure Medical Kits makes Clear Pockets, which have a vinyl window so you can see and locate items easily.

Always keep your kits replenished and filled at home. You will be amazed how this cuts down the stress come packing time, and you'll always be ready to go should a wonderfully unexpected trip come along!

The following packing aids will be helpful:

Organizer bags and pouches
Flat, zippered nylon pouches, or freezer-strength resealable bags are useful both as you pack and on your trip. Stuff sacks can be handy for

travel packs. Both stuff sacks and plastic bags can be used for wet and soiled items.

Core pouch

This organizer is a central part of my "Bundle Method" of packing (see chapter 5) and is a worthwhile investment. The 11 × 16 inch pouch is used to pack wardrobe accessories such as underwear, socks, and hosiery. The Carry-Rite Mini-Organizer (#215) serves as a core pouch that can be hung up in the closet for easy access and is easily found at luggage shops and in some travel stores, such as Easy Going. (For more details, see p. 111.)

Shoe covers

Use old socks or the fabric bags available in luggage and travel stores to protect clothing and shoes. If you use plastic bags, leave them open as shoes need to breathe.

Manila envelopes

Those measuring 9 × 12 or 10 × 13 inches are useful for sending home brochures, organizing guidebook pages, travel notes, and so on. Pre-address them!

Laundry bag

Use a pillow case, an Over-the-Door Neat Net, a plastic garbage bag, or an expandable tote.

1-ounce, 2-ounce, and 4-ounce plastic bottles

Transfer any products from large containers into high quality 1-ounce, 2-ounce, and 4-ounce plastic bottles, available at good outdoor and travel stores. Bottles with screw-on caps are best. To find out how much you might need, track your consumption before your trip. (Do not forget to take enough contact lens solution—it may be hard to find on the road.) To prevent leaks, leave half an inch of air space at the top of each bottle. Squeeze out the air and close the bottle to create a vacuum. You can also tape the tops and store the bottles in a resealable bag. If you don't want to bother, you can buy trial- and travel-sized products at most drug stores.

Skirt hangers

Take a small one.

Other tips:

▼ Choose foil- and plastic-wrapped nail polish remover, shoe polish, facial cleansers, and moist towelettes. Remove all excess packaging.

▼ If you are carrying toilet paper, take only half a roll and remove the inner tube.

▼ Transfer general nonprescription drugs and lozenges (such as headache pills and vitamins) into small, clear, rinsed-out plastic film canisters (available at photo developing centers) or small, previously used pill bottles. Label them with masking tape or stick-on labels. Or, you can buy dose containers from drugstores made in a variety of styles by E-Z Dose.

▼ Prescription drugs must remain in their original containers. Have the doctor prescribe them in two small bottles. Pack one set in your daybag and one in your suitcase.

▼ Film canisters can also be used for putting together a sewing kit and for carrying any little odds and ends you need. (Clear ones are more convenient as you can see what's in them immediately.)

▼ Health and Comfort

Following is a checklist for items that will keep you comfortable and healthy as you travel. Think about each one in view of your destination, mode of travel, and personal needs.

MEDICAL NEEDS

☐ two complete sets of prescription medicine in small bottles, one for your daybag and one for your main bag

☐ a 3 × 5-inch card with your doctor's name and number, your medical history, and a list of allergies

☐ insulated bag for medicine, if needed

☐ nonprescription medications (such as acetaminophen, aspirin, ibuprofen, antacid, anti-diarrheal, laxative, antihistamine, decongestant tablets, cold or flu relief, throat lozenges, fungus treatment cream, vitamins, sleeping pills, etc.)

- ☐ collapsible drinking cup
- ☐ other _____
- ☐ other _____

EYECARE

- ☐ glasses, sunglasses, neck strap, cases
- ☐ your most recently replaced pair of glasses as a backup
- ☐ eyeglass repair kit
- ☐ 2 pairs of contact lenses
- ☐ contact lens kit or sterilizer
- ☐ contact lens solution
- ☐ eyewash for air travel and/or dusty conditions

OUTDOOR PROTECTION

- ☐ sunscreen
- ☐ lip balm
- ☐ hat, visor, or bandanna
- ☐ insect repellent (see below)
- ☐ 1% hydrocortisone cream or anti-itch balm
- ☐ mosquito netting, if needed (see below)

FOOD AND WATER

- ☐ water/water bottle or flask
- ☐ energy snacks (energy bars/trail mix/crackers/fruit/candy/jerky/etc.)
- ☐ water purification equipment or tablets, if needed (see below)

ON THE ROAD

- ☐ jet lag remedy (see below)
- ☐ motion sickness medication or aid (see below)
- ☐ remedy for ear discomfort during takeoff/landing (see below)

- ☐ ear plugs (see below)
- ☐ eyeshades
- ☐ sleep sheets (see below)
- ☐ travel pillow (see below)
- ☐ spritz bottle or facial mister
- ☐ other _____
- ☐ other _____

Insect repellent and mosquito netting — N,N-Diethyl metatolu-amide, or "Deet," is the main chemical ingredient in insect repellents, which vary in strength and come as sprays, liquids, or solid roll-ons. Those containing 12 percent to a maximum of 35 percent are recommended. *Choose a low dosage for children.* Skedaddle insect repellent for children is 17.5-percent Deet.

If you do not want to use a chemical, try natural citronella products. Insect protection can range from simply preventing bites to preventing malaria in many areas of the world. If you are going to a malaria-infested destination, take repellent, mosquito netting or head-net (some are treated with added repellents), and clothing that offers complete coverage. Also find out what vaccinations you need from your physician or the Centers for Disease Control and get the shots six to eight weeks before you leave, since some require repetition.

Water bottle or flask — I always carry water when I travel. Remaining hydrated keeps you energetic and healthy as your body undergoes the stress of new environments, especially hot or dry ones. The smallest flask should hold at least 6 ounces; the largest, up to 1 liter. You can reuse screw-top commercial water bottles or buy flat-shaped flasks. New collapsible plastic pouches allow for easy packing and carrying. The Flexi Flask is even boilable for water purification. If you plan to take drink mixes or prepare purified water, get a wide-mouth water bottle. I especially like totebags and daypacks which feature a water bottle holder on the outside. Look for them in outdoor stores.

Water purification equipment — Traveler's diarrhea, hepatitis A, cholera, shigella, giardia, and salmonella can all be contracted by drinking the local water supply in many countries. To protect yourself, make sure you have some form of water purification with you. For emergency purposes, carry Potable Aqua: iodine-based, chlorine-free tablets that come in a small bottle an inch and a half high. Add one tablet (two if giardia is suspected) to one quart or liter of water, wait three minutes, shake the bottle, and wait ten more minutes before drinking the water (for giardia wait twenty minutes). Designed for emergencies, iodine should not be used on a continuous basis.

For continuous use, the PUR Voyageur provides the highest level of protection and is still portable enough to pack easily. The purifier is an 11 oz., $6^1/_2$-inch long and 2-inch wide cylindrical pump which processes up to 1 liter per minute. A microfilter removes all protozoa (such as giardia cysts) that are larger than on micron, and a tri-iodine resin kills any smaller bacteria and viruses on contact. The result is microbiologically safe drinking water. The replaceable cartridge lasts for 100 gallons, or 1600 cups of water. A carbon cartridge removes chemicals and unpleasant tastes.

Adventure travelers who drink from a fresh water source may prefer the PUR Scout Purifier. It offers the same level of safety as the Voyageur, destroying protozoa, bacteria, and viruses, but it also has an elaborate prefiltration and anti-clog system to deal with mud and other sediments. The PUR Explorer is great for families and larger groups as it processes 1.5 liters per minute.

Other manufacturers of good water purification systems for travel are Sweetwater and Katadyn. Sweetwater's Guardian+Plus Purifier includes a separate Viral Guard filter that can be removed if your trip does not include the threat of virus, and put back when it does.

Another water purification product is the PurLife Personal Water Filtration System. Incredibly, this is an 18 oz. plastic sport bottle that holds a special filter in its cap. You simply fill the bottle, replace the cap, and drink. This bottle fills from any water supply and removes giardia, cryptospridium, virus, chlorine, lead, and heavy metals. Also comes in a model in which you drink from a straw. The filter processes 1800 refills or 300 gallons before you need a replacement filter. This is great for at home, for daily or emergency use, as well as travel.

All of these purifiers are approved by the USEPA.

Don't forget, you can always boil water if you have the opportunity.

Motion sickness medication — This may be medication, an earpatch, or Sea Bands, which are elasticized wristbands that have a hard plastic bump. When the bands are placed on the wrist, the bump presses an acupressure point that controls balance and nausea. Both wristbands must be worn. People who use these bands swear by them.

Ear pressure remedy — Many travelers experience ear discomfort during takeoffs and landings. If you have a cold, allergies, or a sinus condition, the pain is exacerbated. Earplanes disposable earplugs reduce the pain. These plugs have a hole in them and a CeramX filter. They are simply inserted into the ears before takeoff and removed when the airplane arrives at the gate and the cabin door is opened. They are available in adult and children's sizes.

COMFORT NEEDS

Rest and sleep are necessities, not luxuries, when you are traveling. Consider items like travel pillows carefully, even if they seem like "extras."

Travel pillow, eyeshade — Your own travel pillow will help you sleep in any hotel room, campground, train, or bus. Look for a durable, washable one. Crescent-shaped, inflatable neck pillows with washable twill covers are made by Better Sleep. Down and feather versions can be bought at outdoor stores. Although it takes up a lot of space, the fleece-covered Bucky Pillow is incredible—it feels like a pillow and teddy bear rolled into one.

Jet lag remedy — If you've ever suffered from the effects of jet lag you should know about this new product. Originally developed in New Zealand, No Jet Lag is a unique homeopathic remedy constituted of natural herbs which alleviate the symptoms of jet lag. Its effectiveness had been clinically proven and is recognized internationally by business travelers, sports teams, tour operators and airline personnel. I always use this product myself and have arrived alert both at destination and at home.

Ear plugs — Earplugs are invaluable if you land in a noisy hotel. A good brand is the foam-type E.A.R. If you are extraordinarily sensitive to noise, you might want to consider a Marsona Sound Conditioner. This small electronic device drowns out background noise with the soothing sounds of rain or a waterfall. It comes in single or dual voltages and weighs about a pound. This is unquestionably a luxury for most of us, but it might be indispensable for some people.

FIRST-AID/HEALTH KIT

First-aid kits are very personal and differ by individual, destination, and level of protection desired. Below are basic suggestions for general travel. For more information read *Backcountry First Aid* by Buck Tilton (ICS Books), *The Pocket Doctor* by Stephen Bezruchka (Mountaineers), or *Wilderness and Travel Medicine* by Eric A. Weiss. Excellent ready-made first-aid kits for travelers are assembled by Adventure Medical Kits, Atwater Carey, Ltd., and Outdoor Research (physician-owned). These are available at travel and outdoor stores. For those interested in alternative curatives, The Herbal Medicine Kit offers new-age remedies alongside traditional ones (call (800)324-3517).

This kit will handle most minor health problems:

☐ medical items from previous list

☐ antiseptic pads

☐ antibiotic ointment for bites, cuts, sunburns

☐ surgical tape

☐ gauze bandages/pads

☐ Band-Aids

☐ small scissors (if not on your pocketknife)

☐ tweezers or needle (if not on your pocketknife)

☐ moleskin or Instant Skin (a medicated aerosol)

☐ other _____

Consider these for maximum protection:

☐ emergency first-aid handbook (pocketed)

☐ thermometer (nonmercury type for air travel)

- [ ] emergency dental kit (see resources)
- [ ] latex gloves (or nitrile/nonlatex, if allergic to latex)
- [ ] Ace bandage with clips
- [ ] cold compress
- [ ] flushing syringe for wound irrigation
- [ ] emergency blanket
- [ ] antibiotics, prescription (see note below)
- [ ] other _____

Note: You might want to bring antibiotics or your own needle and syringe if you are going to a very remote area where they may not be available. Check with your doctor.

Toiletries/Personal Items

Choose toiletries carefully and remember that many items will be available at your destination.

I can't say enough about Packtowls. This single item is much more useful that any terrycloth towel. It is a piece of feltlike material called viscose that can hold up to ten times its weight in moisture. Compact and lightweight, it works equally well damp or dry. This quick-drying towel does not fray or pill and is machine- or hand-washable. You can use it as a washcloth or towel; as a dish cloth, sponge, potholder, or napkin; or as a headband or dust mask. It is also useful as an emergency compress, bandage, or tourniquet; as an ankle or splint wrap; or as a marker or flag. I have cut one up into small washcloths and kept them damp in a Ziploc bag to use instead of moist towelettes. If you're traveling with kids, they are invaluable. They come in three sizes: standard, the middle-sized Aquatowl, and the bath-sized Megatowl. Bandannas are also useful, as are large handkerchiefs.

Keep your makeup to a minimum by choosing small sample containers or transferring cosmetics to small jars. When you have only one color combination in your wardrobe, one set of makeup is enough, with lipstick to match your accent or brightest color and eyeshadow, eyeliner, and mascara to match your neutral color. Note: If you will be in a hot climate, take lip pencils. Unlike lipsticks, they do not melt.

Leave personal appliances such as hairdryers home if at all possible, because they are bulky. Call ahead to check availability at hotels. (For more on electrical appliances, see p. 62.) For international travel, take a small, dual-voltage dryer with adapters or a single-voltage model with a high-wattage converter and adapters. Consider an easy-care haircut instead. If you need a curling iron, take one that uses butane, or a dual-voltage iron with adapters for international travel. Note: Butane cartridges cannot be carried on airlines.

It never hurts to carry a small roll of toilet paper (remove the inner core) or a packet of Kleenex with you, and I've been in places where, *thank goodness*, I had seat covers. Foil-wrapped moist towelettes, baby wipes, antibacterial wipes, and so on can be helpful, especially if you are traveling with children. Feminine sanitary products are available worldwide, but U.S. brands are very expensive when purchased abroad. If you don't want to pay extra, take enough tampons or sanitary napkins with you for the entire trip. The O.B. brand is compact. Women can use panty liners in underwear to cut down on laundry.

Women traveling abroad or camping may want to consider bringing a urinary director device. Freshette is a palm-sized, reusable, lightweight plastic device that enables women to urinate while standing with minimal undressing. It is available at REI and other outdoor stores. Le Funelle is the same type of product in disposable form and is stocked by travel specialty shops.

For light travel, take only the essentials:

- ☐ shampoo/conditioner (try two-in-one brands)
- ☐ soap or multi purpose travel soap
- ☐ facial cleanser/toner
- ☐ moisturizer
- ☐ antiperspirant
- ☐ body powder/bath salts
- ☐ dental supplies—toothbrush with cap or holder/toothpaste/dental floss/mouthwash
- ☐ shaving supplies—razor/blades/electric shaver/shaving cream/aftershave

- [ ] hair supplies—comb/folding hairbrush/gel/hairspray/mousse/clips/hair ties
- [ ] manicure items—nail clipper/nail file/nail polish/polish remover pads/nailbrush
- [ ] clear nail polish (for runs in nylons)
- [ ] Packtowl or lightweight terrycloth towel
- [ ] washcloth
- [ ] curling iron/hair dryer/etc.

HYGIENE SUPPLIES

- [ ] toilet paper and seat covers
- [ ] moist towelette packets or antibacterial gel
- [ ] feminine sanitary items
- [ ] Freshette or Le Funelle urinary director (for women)
- [ ] contraceptives/condoms
- [ ] other _____

SHOE/FOOTCARE

- [ ] footcream
- [ ] moleskin or 2nd Skin
- [ ] removable insoles and other shoe supplies
- [ ] other _____

▼ Room and Security

Do not depend on the hotel's wake-up call. Bring a compact clock that is easy to see at night and easily set. I like bright-colored models (such as red or white) because they are less likely to be forgotten when you are packing hurriedly. For more on security, see chapter 10.

- [ ] travel alarm clock or wristwatch with alarm
- [ ] small, good flashlight (with extra batteries and bulb for long trip)
- [ ] night light, fluorescent tape for marking light switches, or light-sticks (good for brownouts or blackouts)

- ☐ portable door lock or rubber doorstop
- ☐ portable "hands-free" reading light with extra batteries and bulb
- ☐ intruder alarm
- ☐ duct tape for making repairs along the way
- ☐ a film canister filled with safety pins, nails, screws, etc.
- ☐ portable smoke alarm
- ☐ extension cord
- ☐ sleep sheets for youth hostels (if needed)
- ☐ mini-safe
- ☐ other _____
- ☐ other _____

▼ Clothing Care

By picking packable fabrics and using the Bundle Method of packing (see chapter 5) and other wrinkle-removal methods (see pp. 86–87), you can leave your travel iron or steamer at home. Take one if you want extra insurance against wrinkles. Make sure it is dual voltage for international travel.

A steamer is a plastic vessel with a heating element inside. You fill it with water (in some a bit of salt must be added to speed the steaming), plug it in, and in about five minutes, you will have a supply of hot steam that lasts between eight and twelve minutes. Hang up your garment and glide the steamer along to coax the wrinkles out. Steamers are wonderful for removing travel wrinkles in light- and medium-weight fabrics. They weigh much less than irons do, and you can hang the garment up anywhere to steam it. Steamers cannot, however, set a crease in slacks or put the crispness back in a skirt, shirt, or jacket. To do this you need the weight and heat provided by an iron. Do not expect the same performance from a travel iron as you get from your iron at home. It lacks the weight and heating ability. Still, high-quality models will work well on the road.

Some works-in-a-pinch alternatives to these appliances are Wrinkle Free and Lewis N. Clark Wrinkle Remover, which are sprays that act as fabric relaxers on all fabrics except 100-percent polyester and silk. You spray the garment and use your hand to smooth out wrinkles.

You can buy or make a tiny sewing kit. Include in a clear plastic film canister: needles, straight pins inserted into a small piece of fabric, thread wrapped around a small piece of cardboard, a thimble, several sizes of safety pins, and some basic buttons. You can reinforce the stitching on buttons and sew an extra button on the inside of each garment before you go. A small roll of Scotch tape will make an emergency hem.

If you plan to handwash clothes on your trip, you will want to bring some or all of the laundry items on the list below. For tips on cleaning clothes while traveling (and explanations for some of these items), see pp. 85–88.

Multipurpose travel soap or detergent is sold as a liquid in a squeeze bottle, in dry packets, or as a solid. You'll find it in travel and outdoor stores. For a clothesline, take the elasticized braided Flexoline, which does not need clips to hang most items, or 10 feet of nylon cord. Take one or two inflatable hangers for drying blouses and delicates quickly. A sink stopper—the flat, round type—can be helpful; these are often missing from sinks and tubs. For a laundry sack, you can use a plastic bag, a pillow case, or an Over-the-Door Neat Net bag, which is available at Toys R Us.

If you want to be prepared for stains, take one of these:

▼ A small solid stick or tube of liquid laundry pretreat or stain remover. Products for washable fabrics include Cadie, Kiss Off, Magic Wand (good for ball-point ink), Shout, Spray'n Wash, or Zout. They must be laundered out.

▼ A spot remover for *dry-cleanable and washable* fabrics. I recommend Goddard's Nonflammable Dry-Cleaning Solvent or Swiss Care Paste.

▼ Spot-remover pads. These will remove stains such as oil, makeup, ink, blood, and food stains from *nonwashable* but colorfast silk and wool fabrics.

The following items will allow you to wash and maintain your wardrobe; you'll also be ready to do minor repairs and remove stains.

BASIC KIT:

- ☐ sewing kit
- ☐ multipurpose travel soap
- ☐ clothesline
- ☐ inflatable hanger(s)
- ☐ hanger clips for clothesline
- ☐ stain treatment product
- ☐ sink stopper
- ☐ plastic bag for carrying wet or soiled clothing

OPTIONAL ITEMS:

- ☐ Packtowl (for blotting extra moisture)
- ☐ plastic skirt hanger
- ☐ detergent packets (dry)
- ☐ cold-water soap packets (dry)
- ☐ shoe-shine pads
- ☐ lint brush (or use Scotch tape)
- ☐ spray-on wrinkle remover
- ☐ stain removal supplies
- ☐ travel iron or steamer (and salt if necessary)

▼ Entertainment

These are extra things that make travel a little more enjoyable. Take what you have room for. (See pp. 8 and 62 for advice on electronics.)

- ☐ books
- ☐ magazines
- ☐ cards, travel games
- ☐ electronic games, recharger, disks
- ☐ portable tape or CD player, headphones, tapes or CDs, and a tape or CD carrying case
- ☐ travel or shortwave radio
- ☐ microcassette recorder, headphones, and tapes

- [ ] jump rope, inflatable beach ball, exercise bands
- [ ] musical instrument
- [ ] other _____

▼ Sightseeing and Photography

Guidebooks and maps greatly enhance a trip but paper is heavy. To cut down, research thoroughly in advance, and photocopy on both sides of the paper those pages you need for your itinerary. You can enlarge or reduce them, cut off the margins, and staple sheets together. Organize them in labeled manila envelopes, for example, Italy, France, and so on. After you use them, give them away to other travelers, fill the empty envelopes with brochures and other memorabilia that you have collected, and mail those home periodically.

Minolta makes ultra-compact binoculars that are smaller than a cassette tape and weigh less than six ounces. They can be used indoors or out, close and detailed, or far and wide. They come in two models: 6 × 18 or 8 × 18 magnification (see Easy Going listing in Resources).

CARRYING FILM

Label each canister with a stick-on dot and give it a number. In your notebook record the number, then list the shots you take. You will know what it is when you get home.

You can buy prepaid Kodak processing mailers from your local Kodak dealers if you want to send film back to the United States as you go. For more information, call Kodak at (800) 345-6971. Note: Prepaid mailers are best used only from the United States and Europe. I have heard many reports of film lost in transit from Asian, Latin-American, and Pacific countries. Use your best judgment and ask fellow travelers of their experiences in mailing film home.

For film inspection at the airport, place your film in plastic resealable bags and always ask (politely) for hand inspection to avoid the X-ray machine. Kodak recommends that you do not use commercially available lead-lined bags. They are an invitation to have the X-ray machine turned up. If your camera has film in it, always ask for that, too, to be inspected by hand.

Keep all cameras and camcorders loaded with batteries and able to function upon request during inspections. Cameras that do not function can be viewed as security risks, leading to delays in passing customs.

The following list will help you equip yourself for most sightseeing ventures.

- ☐ maps and guides, or reduced, photocopied pages from these in labeled 9 × 12-inch manila envelopes (this saves a lot of weight!)
- ☐ magnifier (flat plastic type) or combo flash light/magnifier
- ☐ compass
- ☐ travel diary, ledger, or small spiral notebooks
- ☐ pens
- ☐ clips to keep papers together
- ☐ camera, plenty of film, flash
- ☐ filters, lenses
- ☐ dustbag to protect equipment (e.g., pillowcase)
- ☐ film cooler with synthetic ice for hot climates
- ☐ extra batteries for camera and flash
- ☐ prepaid film processing mailing envelopes
- ☐ lens cleaner kit
- ☐ video camera, tapes, recharger
- ☐ camera bag, fanny pack, pouch
- ☐ binoculars or opera glasses
- ☐ other _____

▼ Miscellaneous Gear

Eating/Drinking

You may want to bring the following if you will be picnicking or taking care of some of your own meals and you're unsure of what kitchen equipment will be available to you. A Swiss Army knife or similar pocketknife is essential. They come fitted with a variety of tools.

Choose the smallest one that has what you really need: a knife, a bottle opener, a can opener, and a corkscrew. Other tools such as tweezers, saw-tooth blades, scissors, and magnifiers are also useful.

The weight of a travel coffee maker makes it worthwhile only for coffee die-hards. If you are going abroad, make sure the coffee maker is a dual-voltage appliance or that you have a converter and the right adapters.

- ☐ flask or water bottle
- ☐ food or snacks (dried fruit, dried soup, energy bars, jerky, etc.)
- ☐ pocket knife
- ☐ bottle, jar, can opener, corkscrew (if not on your pocketknife)
- ☐ spoon (you can eat almost anything with a spoon and a pocketknife)

Extras:

- ☐ hot/cold cup
- ☐ travel coffee maker
- ☐ utensil set (plastic plate, fork, knife, spoon)
- ☐ beverage coil heater (dual-voltage for foreign travel)
- ☐ small cutting board
- ☐ Packtowl, wipe-up cloth, or moist towelettes
- ☐ bottle stopper
- ☐ multi purpose travel soap
- ☐ insulated cooler bag (foldable)
- ☐ tablecloth or large bandanna
- ☐ packets of tea/coffee
- ☐ salt, pepper, spices, condiments
- ☐ liquor (with vodka and an eyedropper you can also disinfect utensils)
- ☐ extra cork/bottle stopper
- ☐ other _____

Shopping

You can use your regular pocket calculator for currency exchange, but Money Exchange Calculators make handling financial and numerical transactions a breeze. In addition to calculating currency exchanges, they will change centimeters into inches, kilometers into miles, and Celsius into Fahrenheit. For information on shopping and shipping, See chapter 11.

- ☐ string bag, or use your expandable totebag or daypack
- ☐ pocket calculator or currency exchange calculator
- ☐ tape measure
- ☐ magnifying glass (for inspecting jewelry, art, and so on)
- ☐ gift list (with sizes of friends and family members)
- ☐ mailing supplies: mailing tape, bubble wrap, scissors
- ☐ other _____

Conversation Starters for Foreign Travel

These may be the most important items in your suitcase. They will help you connect with local people.

- ☐ pictures of your home and family (in plastic cover)
- ☐ language phrasebooks, dictionaries, electronic language translator
- ☐ small gifts/postcards from the United States
- ☐ other _____

Office Supplies

Remove all packaging and store your supplies in a nylon pouch or Ziploc bag. You may be able to find a small portable office kit that includes many of the items listed here.

- ☐ addresses or electronic organizer
- ☐ notebook or travel journal

- ☐ business cards, calling cards
- ☐ extra stationery and other writing paper, postcards, envelopes
- ☐ Scotch tape
- ☐ Post-its
- ☐ rubber bands
- ☐ paper clips, multiclips
- ☐ small stapler, staples
- ☐ pens
- ☐ permanent marker/highlighter
- ☐ 10 × 13-inch mailing envelopes
- ☐ shipping supplies
- ☐ other _____

Computer and Telephone Equipment

For complete information on mobile computing needs, log on to www.teleadapt.com.

- ☐ cellular phone, charger, battery pack
- ☐ modem tele-coupler and foreign phone jack adapters or other connectivity equipment
- ☐ extra diskettes
- ☐ battery charger
- ☐ battery pack(s)
- ☐ converter, adapter, surge protector
- ☐ screen cleaning pads
- ☐ computer tool kit
- ☐ telephone calling card
- ☐ other _____

▼ World Guide to Voltages and Outlet Types

Many countries require more than one type of plug. Below are the most commonly found types. For a description of the letter codes, see p. 63.

Afghanistan – B/D	Chile – D	Greenland – D
Albania – D	China – B/C/D/E	Grenada – B/C/D
Algeria* – D	CIS (former USSR) – D	Guadeloupe – D
Angola – B/D	Colombia* – A/D	Guam* – A
Antigua – A/B/C	Congo – D	Guatemala* – A
Argentina – C/D/E	Cook Islands – E	Guinea – D
Armenia – D	Costa Rica* – A/C	Guyana* – A/B/C/D
Australia – E	Croatia – D	Haiti* – A
Austria – D	Cuba* – A	Honduras* – A
Azores – B/D	Cyprus - B/C	Hong Kong – C
Bahamas* – A	Czechoslovakia – B/D	Hungary – D
Bahrain – B/C	Denmark – D	Iceland – B/C/D
Bangladesh – B/D	Dominica – B/C	India – B/C/D
Barbados* – A	Dominican Rep.* – A	Indonesia* – B/D
Belgium – B/D	Ecuador* – A/D	Iran – D
Belize* – A	Egypt – B/C/D	Iraq – B/C/D
Bermuda* – A/C/E	El Salvador* – A	Ireland – B/C
Bhutan – C/D	England – B/C/D	Israel – D/E
Bolivia* – A/B/D	Equatorial Guinea – D	Italy – D
Bosnia-Herzegovina – D	Estonia – D	Ivory Coast – B/D
Botswana – B/C	Ethiopia – D	Jamaica* – A/D
Brazil* – A/D	Fiji – E	Japan* – A
Brunei – B/C	Finland – D	Jordan – B/C/D
Bulgaria – D	France – D	Kampuchea – D
Burma (Myanmar) – B/C/D	French Guiana – B/D	Kazakhstan – D
Burundi – B/D	French Polynesia* – A/D	Kenya – B/C
Cameroon* – B/D	Gabon – C/D	Korea (N and S) – A/D
Canada* – A/C	Gambia, The – B/C	Kuwait – B/C/D
Canary Islands – D	Germany – B/D	Laos – A/D
Cayman Islands* – A	Ghana – B/C/D	Latvia – D
Central African Rep. – B/D	Gibraltar – B/C/D	Lebanon* – D
Chad – D	Greece – B/D	Lesotho – B/D

* 110 volts or a combination of 110 volts and 220 volts; all others 220 volts

† denotes plug unique to country

Liberia* – A/B/C	Norway – D	Suriname* – D
Libya* – B/D	Okinawa* – A	Swaziland – B/D
Liechtenstein – D	Oman – B/C	Sweden – D
Lithuania – D	Pakistan – B/D	Switzerland – B/D
Luxembourg – D	Panama* – A/E	Syria – B/D
Macao – B/D	Papua New Guinea – A/E	Tahiti – A
Macedonia – D	Paraguay – D	Taiwan* – A
Madagascar* – D	Peru* – A/D	Tanzania – B/C
Madeira - B/D	Philippines* – A/D	Thailand – A/D
Majorca – B/D	Poland – D	Togo* – D
Malagasy – D	Portugal – B/D	Tonga – D/E
Malawi – B/C	Puerto Rico* – A	Trinidad/Tobago* – A/B/C
Malaysia – B/C	Qatar – B/C	Tunisia* – D
Maldives – D	Romania – D	Turkey – D
Mali – D	Russia – D	Turkmenistan – D
Malta – B/C	Rwanda – D	Uganda – B/C
Martinique* – B/D	St. Kitts-Nevis – B/C	Ukraine – D
Mauritania – D	St. Lucia – B/C	United Arab Emir. – B/C
Mauritius – B/C/D	St. Maarten* – D	United States* – A
Mexico* – A	St. Vincent – B/C	Upper Volta – D
Micronesia* – A	Samoa, Amer.* – A/D/E	Uruguay – C/D/E
Moldova – D	Samoa, West – E	USSR (former) – D
Monaco* – D	Saudi Arabia* – A/B/D	Uzbekistan – D
Mongolia – D	Scotland – B/C	Vanatu – C/D/E
Morocco* – D	Senegal* – D	Venezuela* – A
Mozambique – D/B	Seychelles – B/C	Vietnam* – A/D
Namibia – D	Sierra Leone – B/C/D	Virgin Is. (Amer.)* – A
Nepal – B/D	Singapore – B/C/D	Virgin Is. (Brit.) – B/C
Netherlands – D	Slovakia – D	Wales – B/C
Neth. Antilles* – A/B/C	Slovenia – D	Yemen – A/B/C/D
New Caledonia – A/D	Solomon Islands – E	Yugoslavia (former) – D
New Hebrides – E	Somalia – B/C/D	Zaire – D
New Zealand – E	South Africa, Rep. of† – C	Zambia – B/C
Nicaragua* – A	Spain* – A/D	Zimbabwe – B/C
Niger – B/D	Sri Lanka – B/D	
Nigeria – B/D	Sudan – B/C/D	

* 110 volts or a combination of 110 volts and 220 volts; all others 220 volts
† denotes plug unique to country

▼ Electrical Appliances

Traveling with electrical appliances can be a nuisance because they are heavy and bulky. Do you really need that hairdryer or iron? If you do, pack the smallest, lightest model (dual-voltage for foreign travel) you can find, with the right adapter plug(s) if you will be out of the country.

Choosing the right electrical configuration for your appliance can be complex. To be able to use the appliance for foreign travel, you will need an adapter plug because outlets abroad are all different. If your appliance is not dual-voltage you may also need a voltage converter or transformer. Consult a specialty travel store, luggage store, or merchant specializing in electrical merchandise who is familiar with foreign travel and the equipment you might need. Below is a guide to familiarize yourself with the subject.

Most Common Adapter Plugs

ADAPTER PLUGS

You need adapter plugs for foreign travel for *all* appliances because wall outlets are different in different places. In some countries you will find more than one type of wall socket in the same room! Slip the appropriate adapter onto the plug of your dual-voltage appliance or onto your converter or transformer, then plug it into the wall.

Adapter plugs such as those illustrated above are the most common types. However, other variations do exist, including 3-pronged plugs, with or without a grounding pin.

Check the illustrations above and the World Guide to Voltages and Outlet Types on pp. 60–61 and purchase the right adapter plug(s) for the wall sockets you may encounter. The illustrations correspond to the following adapters for the most commonly found outlets. Please note that they may be named differently by different vendors.

- ▼ Type A – Flat, parallel blades
- ▼ Type B – Fat, round pins
- ▼ Type C – Three rectangular prongs
- ▼ Type D – Thin, round pins (use this plug for recessed outlets)
- ▼ Type E – Flat, angled blades

ADAPTER PLUGS WITH GROUNDING PINS

Adapter plugs with a ground are more difficult to find but they are available from well-stocked travel stores. They slip onto the three-pronged grounded American plug. There are different grounding plugs for different countries.

CONVERTERS AND TRANSFORMERS

A converter or transformer allows your 110 volt (single-voltage) appliance to run on the 220- or 240-volt current found in many foreign countries. (Some countries, such as Japan and Mexico, run on 110 volts, as we do.) Others may use both 110 volts and 220 volts! If you have dual-voltage appliances, you do not need a converter. All you need to do is buy the adapter plug(s) and adjust the voltage on the appliance.

Most converters and low-wattage transformers are designed for intermittent use. Using them continuously may cause the appliance to wear out quickly. Because American appliances are run on 60 cycles and foreign appliances on 50 cycles, your appliance may not work as fast even with a transformer. Hairdryers should be set on low to avoid overheating. Some models have safety locks that disable the high speed when they are used on 220 or 240 volts.

Transformers for sustained use, as with computers, modems, printers, sewing machines, cassette players, etc., are available. See next page under "heavy-duty transformers."

SINGLE-VOLTAGE APPLIANCES

If you have a single-voltage appliance, read below to determine what kind of converter or transformer you need. There are two types of converters: high-wattage and low-wattage. The one you need depends on how many watts your appliance uses and what type of appliance you have. Note that converters for these two types of appliances are *not* interchangeable.

High-wattage converters (between 50 and 1600 watts) — These are required for heat-producing appliances such as hairdryers, irons, steamers, food or bottle warmers, travel coffee makers, curling irons, and heating coils for beverages.

Low-wattage converters (up to 50 watts) — These are for electronic or *motorized* appliances such as battery rechargers, shavers, contact lens sterilizers, strobes, flashes, massagers, radios, calculators, tape recorders and cassette players, sound conditioners (white noise machines), and video camcorders. Converters for electronic or motorized appliances are also called transformers.

To select a converter:

1. Determine if yours is a heat-producing appliance or a motorized, electronic appliance.
2. Determine the wattage consumption and cycle ratings. They are usually indicated on the item. Always check the actual wattage consumption of the unit to get the proper size of transformer.

OTHER GADGETS YOU MAY NEED

Battery eliminator — This device will let you plug your battery-operated appliance, such as a personal tape player, cassette player, or radio (if it has a DC jack), into the wall instead of consuming an endless amount of batteries.

A "reverse" transformer — A device that enables you to use a foreign 220- or 240-volt motorized, electronic appliance (up to 50 watts) on North American 110-volt current. These transformers are useful for visitors to our country and for those things you picked up while traveling. These will not work on heat-producing appliances, such as hairdryers.

A heavy-duty transformer — If your equipment's wattage consumption exceeds the ratings of the small converters, you will then need heavy-duty transformers. These are also necessary for continuous use (more than 30 minutes at a time), e.g., small and large computers, modems, and printers, regardless of wattage consumption listed on the appliance.

Always check the exact consumption to select the right transformer. A good rule of thumb is to double the level. For example, if your appliance is 100 watts, choose a transformer that is 200 watts. Transformers come in 200-, 300-, 500-, 750-, and 1,000-watt sizes and are available in electrical shops, from specialty relocation merchants, and in well-stocked travel stores (see Resources). Powerful transformers are large and very heavy. Think twice before taking one along.

Motorized, electronic appliances that require large transformers include computers, printers, modems, and photocopiers, as well as large radios, stereos, tape decks, large and small food mixers, food processors, blenders, sewing machines, refrigerators, power drills, large medical devices, and typewriters. Many small computers and laptop and notebook computers come in dual-voltage models. If they are not dual-voltage, check the wattage for the right size transformer but remember that for use over 30 minutes to an hour, a heavy-duty transformer is recommended. Fax machines do not work reliably even with a transformer. Heat-producing appliances that may require larger transformers include electric blankets, large coffee makers, percolators, and large hot plates.

Some appliances are useless abroad because they only run on 110-volt current; among them are television sets, VCRs, microwave ovens, and clock radios.

Lamps — Because of bulb and wiring differences, it is best to either buy a desk lamp overseas or purchase a battery-operated reading light, such as Beam and Read. Some models have an optional dual-voltage transformer which can be connected to the lamp and plugged into an outlet with the appropriate adapter plug, to cut down on battery consumption. If you plan to use this to read in bed, an extension cord may be handy to pack.

Mobile computing equipment — Different countries have different types of phone jacks! If you need to plug in your modem, you may need a foreign phone jack adapter. Check with a well-stocked travel store (see Resources).

Or, get the Road Warriors Tele-Travel Kit International, which includes a high-speed tele-coupler, a full set of telephone jack adapters, and electrical adapters. Available at your computer store or from AR Industries (by phone at (800) 274-4277 ext. 731 or online at www.warrior.com). Another complete website for mobile computing is Teleadapt www.teleadapt.com. They will tell you about all the problems you might be faced with and how to solve them.

4

The Carry-on Wardrobe

If you want to go carry-on instead of hauling lots of bags, you have to choose your wardrobe carefully. Your garments must be packable and, since they are limited, must serve you in a wide variety of social and climatic situations. *Functionality, versatility,* and *style* are your primary considerations. Each may have a different priority depending on the type of trip. The more time you take to refine your wardrobe, the better it will serve you.

▼ How Much to Take

Trips vary in length, climate, activities, and in how mobile and self-sufficient you want to be. Sometimes you want to travel ultra-light, while other times you need more clothing choices and don't care as much about the number of bags you have. I have divided wardrobe plans into three approaches and one hybrid. For each trip, pick a packing approach that matches your activities, climate, and mobility and self-sufficiency levels.

The Minimalist Approach

The minimalist travels light. The wash-and-wear wardrobe is perfect for warm weather, for short trips (between three and five days), and for single-purpose trips that are entirely casual or entirely business. You will be washing often and wearing the same outfits frequently. What you need will fit into the smaller 20-inch-long commuter carry-on, and the advantage is incredible mobility; you will easily be able to carry all of your luggage on any kind of public transportation.

The Moderate Approach

Most carry-on travelers will take the moderate approach. A basic travel wardrobe of eight or nine pieces will prepare you for temperature swings and varying activities. Your laundry schedule will be somewhat relaxed. You will have several choices for day and evening, an advantage if you will be with the same people continually and would like some variety in your wardrobe. The moderate wardrobe is the most that many people can fit comfortably in a carry-on.

The Luxury Approach

For those who prefer to have available as many options in clothing and accessories as possible, the luxury approach is the one to choose. You may be going to formal or business events that require certain types of clothing. You may need to prepare for very cold weather or special activities. The extra convenience may justify a heavier suitcase or even a second bag.

The Multipurpose Approach

Assume that your trip requires two distinct wardrobes: one for cold weather, one for warm; or one for business and one for casual. How do you pack for two purposes in a single carry-on? The answer is to pack two minimalist wardrobes (or one minimalist and one moderate), one for each segment of your trip. The three-compartment carry-on is the best bag for such trips. Pack two wardrobes, each in its own compartment, and use the third compartment for toiletries (see chapter 5 for packing instructions).

▼ Clothing Guidelines

Whatever the purpose of the trip, you can assemble a good travel wardrobe by keeping a few guidelines in mind:

- ▼ Take only comfortable clothes, choosing garments that will accommodate a security wallet.
- ▼ Select versatile garments in simple styles.
- ▼ Select compact, easily maintained fabrics.
- ▼ Pack separates.

- ▼ Choose a color scheme and stick to it.
- ▼ Pack clothing that can be layered, rather than bulky garments.
- ▼ Respect local customs.

Meet all these conditions and your clothes will easily go in a carry-on bag!

Such clothes do exist and finding them is a matter of thinking about the requirements and making good choices: simple styles are more likely to be appropriate and not bulky, separates are versatile and comfortable, comfortable clothing is likely to be easily maintained and offer room for a security wallet, and a color scheme and separates will make your wardrobe versatile. This is what this chapter is all about. In it, we will consider the guidelines and the various garments that you will be taking.

Comfort

We often give up comfort for fashion's sake. Don't! Choose loose-fitting garments and cushioned, broken-in shoes. Loose-fitting clothes will accommodate under-garment security wallets.

For extended plane, car, and bus travel, wear comfortable, roomy garments that breathe, such as knits. Loose-fitting skirts or pants with elasticized or drawstring waistbands and shoes that leave room for expanded feet are essential. Take a pair of soft folding slippers, thongs, or thick socks to wear during the flight.

Even if you are a minimalist, you can add a "travel day" outfit to the wardrobe list: a skirt or comfortable pair of pants, and a shirt. You can also wear your principal jacket, skirt, and blouse. Your sweater can remain in your main bag or daybag.

If you are a moderate or luxury traveler, choose any garment combination you plan to take. Wear the heaviest items to reduce your packing load. If you are traveling from a cold climate to a hot one, dress for arrival, not departure. Do not arrive in Hawaii at Christmas in your overcoat!

The Color Scheme

Start with a color scheme. Space is too valuable to be wasted on odd pieces of clothing that cannot be combined with other items. The practical travel wardrobe consists of separates revolving around one basic, neutral color scheme. This allows you to mix and match items freely to create different looks. Use a shirt or blouse, scarf, ties, belt, and other accessories to add one or two accent colors. Choosing a color scheme also limits the number of pairs of shoes you have to bring. Limiting yourself to one color combination gives you a framework for shopping. Color can make you feel good, look good, and create appropriate impressions in all kinds of situations. Items that do not fit in the color scheme simply do not go!

Before you try to decide on particular colors, look over your clothes. Do you see a color pattern that you prefer? Do you have enough items for any one color to form the basis for a wardrobe? Research the customs of the countries you plan to visit. In some countries, it is inappropriate for tourists to wear certain colors that have a particular cultural significance.

Choose lighter colors for warm weather; medium and darker colors for cooler climates and because they show the dirt less. They are safe and versatile in any situation. These colors are also more versatile because they are appropriate for day or evening. Choose neutral tones for the basic pieces of your wardrobe and for warm weather travel. Choose solids rather than prints, except for a two-piece dress and perhaps a blouse. Solids mix and match easily and can be conveniently transformed from day to evening, from casual to fancy. For shirts, blouses, sweaters, and accessories, you can choose from a wider variety of accent colors.

Neutral, seasonless colors:

▼ Blacks—all shades

▼ Gray—silvery-gray, light and medium gray, charcoal gray, and all in between

▼ Neutral beiges—beige, camel, taupe, tan, khaki, cream, ivory, sand

▼ Brown—cocoa, rust, chocolate, smoke brown, and others

▼ Navy—nautical, bright, black navy, royal

If you like to wear a little more color, consider:

▼ Bright neutrals—red, teal, purple, jade

▼ Deep neutrals—forest green, hunter green, deep teal, burgundy, rust, copper, plum, cocoa, tan, taupe, khaki, sage

These colors can be used as accents, too. The following neutrals only work in spring and summer but may be worn as accents all year long:

▼ Pastels, light and dark—pink, yellow, mint green, lavender, peach

▼ White—seasonless in shirts and blouses only; in other pieces, such as jackets, dresses, slacks, and so on, it is for summer only.

The charts on p. 72 show color combinations derived from neutral schemes. Once the basic wardrobe pieces and shoes have been chosen, add other blouses, shirts, shoes, and accessories in coordinating accent colors.

Fabrics

We overpackers are fortunate to live in an era of space-age synthetic fabrics. It is amazing how many of them are comfortable, wrinkle-resistant, fast-drying, attractive, and functional to boot! Take advantage of these fabrics and incorporate them into your wardrobe. Many of them can be found in outdoor and travel stores, or in catalogs.

For casual wear, cotton pants with a wrinkle-resistant finish are made by Eddie Haggar, Jantzen, Dockers, and Cherokee, among others. If it's important that your clothes dry quickly, consider the Supplex nylon and cotton/nylon "travel clothing" offered by companies such as Ex Officio, Travelsmith, Royal Robbins, Tarponwear, Sun Precautions, Railriders, and Sierra Designs.

As far as natural fabrics go, cotton, cotton/polyester, and linen are still preferred choices for summer heat. Just embrace the wrinkles or be prepared for them. Relaxed, open, or mesh weaves are easier to care for than tightly woven fabrics.

For winter cold and for business, choose wool. A year-round weight (9 oz.) will keep you cool when it is hot, and warm when it is cold. Or pack merino knits—comfortable to sleep in! And wool is packing resilient—its fibers recover when you hang it up.

The chart on p. 73 lists recommended travel fabrics. For more details, see Layering.

▼ Wardrobe Color Planner—Women

First neutral color (for jackets, skirts, and slacks)	beige	navy	black	bright	gray
Second neutral color (for shirts, blouses, and sweaters)	navy white or ivory black *casual only:* pastels bright neutrals deep neutrals	neutral beiges white or ivory burgundy gray *casual only:* bright neutrals deep neutrals	white or ivory khaki taupe gray bright neutrals	black white or ivory gray navy neutral beiges	white or ivory black camel navy *casual only:* pink peach yellow
Shoes, belts, and handbags	neutral brown	navy	black gray	black	gray black neutral
Accent colors (for accessories, blouses, jewelry)	earth tones gold ivory bright colors deep colors	red burgundy gold silver bright colors	red gold white ivory silver	silver gold brights white ivory	red burgundy deep green pastels silver gold

▼ Wardrobe Color Planner—Men

First neutral color (for suits, jackets, and slacks)	beige/brown	navy	black	gray
Second neutral color (for shirt and second pair of slacks)	white or ivory brown any other beige	neutral beige white or ivory burgundy gray	gray white or ivory	black navy burgundy
Shoes and belts	brown	black	black	black
Accent colors	earth tones burgundy or red pastels brights deeps	gold red hunter green	red	burgundy red

▼ Recommended Fabrics for Travel Wardrobes

	Cold to mild climates (3-season)	Warm to hot climates
Jackets, skirts, slacks, and shorts *Choose medium- to light-weight fabrics for year-round wearability. Wool gabardine and knits are especially recommended.*	100% wool gabardine wool/synthetic blends 100% polyester (i.e., microfiber) merino wool jersey knits synthetic suede rayon and rayon blends cotton jersey knits, heavier weight viscose blends 100% silk*	lightweight wool gabardine cotton or cotton/polyester knits natural/synthetic blends with linen look viscose and other synthetic blends 100% cotton* cotton/polyester polyester crepe de chine handwashable silk* silk—raw, hopsack, and tweed* supplex nylon linen* tencel/cotton
Sweaters/ warm shirts *Choose medium-to light-weight*	100% wool (angora, cashmere, lambswool, merino, etc.) wool and synthetic blends 100% acrylic cotton/cotton blend knits in heavier weights Polartec fleece/micro fleece wool flannel	100% cotton knits cotton/polyester knits cotton/silk blends cotton/linen blends* cotton chamois or flannel
Shirts/blouses	cotton/synthetic blends polyester crepe de chine rayon and rayon crepe* various synthetic blends silk jacquard and other silks* silklike synthetics	cotton knits cotton/viscose cotton/synthetic blends polyester crepe de chine various natural/synthetic blends 100% cotton* linen* tencel/cotton
Dresses and 2-piece dresses	wool jersey knits wool and synthetic blend knits wool or rayon challis* washable silk and raw silk* cotton knits, heavy weight various synthetic blends (including viscose acetate, etc.)	cotton and cotton blend knits cotton crepe or gauze cotton/polyester blends rayon crepe* linen/synthetic blends various natural/synthetic blends linen* tencel/cotton

* Needs ironing or steaming

Sun Protective Fabrics — Some fabrics reflect or absorb the sun's UV rays, providing some protection for your skin. Among synthetics, tightly woven Supplex nylon is a widely used fabric that reduces exposure. Conventional fabrics include unbleached cottons, high-luster polyesters, thin satiny silk, darker colors, and tightly-woven fabrics like denim and cotton duck (*San Jose Mercury News*, May 31, 1995). Sun Precautions and other catalogs (see Resources) offer clothing and hats that they rate with 30+ SPF. Tarponwear and Ex Officio use a "UPF" (Ultraviolet Protection Rating), obtained by testing fabrics with a spectrophotometer. Important note: though clothes can provide real protection, you should use sunscreen for maximum protection, particularly on exposed areas of the body.

Separates

Separates allow you to mix and match easily and extend the uses of your wardrobe. They are also easier to pack. A two-piece dress, a skirt, and a blouse made of the same fabric in a solid, stripe, or print, can be your most versatile garments. In a knit, washable silk, or rayon crepe, they can be worn for day or evening, for casual or dressy occasions. They can also be mixed and matched with your other items in many combinations. (Dresses are bulkier to pack and limit access to your security wallet. If you must take one, choose a very simple, neutral color chemise or shirtwaist dress in a fabric that can be worn in the day or evening, such as Travelsmith's Indispensible Black Dress.)

Other excellent choices are the unstructured jacket or blazer with ample room for layering; A-line, straight, wrap-around, or not-too-full skirts (with pockets); split skirts; shirts and blouses in scoop-neck, campshirt, turtleneck, button-down, and polo styles; and coordinated knit sweater or jacket sets. All your garments should have pockets.

Multifunctional Garments

Stay away from jumpsuits and dresses that are designed for specific functions. Look at every garment and think of the different ways you can wear it: a large T-shirt can replace a robe, beach cover-up, and sleepwear. Long underwear, cotton tights, and leggings can be worn in bed. A skirt and blouse in the same fabric can be a two-piece dress or two separate outfits. A merino-knit tunic and leggings can be nice enough for a restaurant or slept in on a long bus ride. A simple button-down campshirt can be casual or dressy. Polo shirts are more versatile than conventional T-shirts and protect one's neck from the sun as well. Walking shorts can double as swim trunks. A sweater with gold buttons can be casual or dressy. If it has a V-neck and no pockets, it can also be worn backwards.

Simple Styles

Simplicity will get you by in any situation, casual or dressy. You can also get years of wear out of your wardrobe if you choose classic styles. Simple styles are also easier to pack; drapey skirts and pleats are more difficult and more time-consuming to care for on the road. Also, a classic look guarantees acceptance in most parts of the world, no matter what the custom.

Sleepwear and Loungewear

Nothing feels as comforting after a long day of sightseeing as curling up in your hotel room with a good book. But loungewear and sleepwear consume lots of space. When choosing specific items, keep these tips in mind.

A dress-length T-shirt can be worn as a nightgown and as a swim cover-up, bathrobe, or even a dress (add a nice belt or sash). For insulation, wear long underwear underneath or a turtleneck.

For leg warmth, add silk-, cotton-, or polyester-knit leggings. Athletic leggings can also be worn for exercise.

Sleep in long underwear. Silk- or polyester-knit shirts and leggings will keep you warm and are cozy to wear. Try a medium weight.

If you still want conventional sleepwear, choose, instead of a nightgown and robe, a packable pajama set that looks nice enough to wear down the hall. Check out The Primary Layer catalog (see Resources) for more on pajamas.

Robes take up too much space in a carry-on. Plan on wearing your pajamas, raincoat, or long T-shirt instead.

Maintenance

Choose the type and amount of clothing that you will be able to maintain according to the laundry services available. Are you going to do your own wash? How often? Are there dry cleaners where you are going? Are there laundromats? Take great care in choosing fabrics.

Decide whether you want to lug an iron or steamer. If you do not, stick to wrinkle-resistant, drip-dry, hand washables. Find out about the cost, quality, and availability of dry cleaning before taking lots of dry-clean-only fabrics. Make sure you know how to remove stains (see pp. 222–226) and carry stain-removing supplies with you (see p. 224).

For women, I suggest taking two pairs of removable garment shields. These are perspiration guards that you slip over your bra under your shirt or dress. They will cut your laundry load in half, because you do not have to wash merely because of perspiration. They are available in fabric stores.

Formal Wear or Special Events

Even cruises that have one or two formal evenings no longer require evening gowns and tuxedos; in most cases a silky dress and a coat and tie are the norm. For formal events and evening wear, select elegant packable fabrics such as a silky synthetic, wool knit, rayon crepe, and synthetic blends. Use accessories to add flair.

No matter what packing approach you have chosen, dress-up wear will be limited. For the minimalist traveler, the two-piece dress (or a skirt or slacks and dressy blouse or cardigan) with a bright scarf or belt might be as dressy as you get. Moderate and luxury travelers have a bit more choice in the two-piece dress and another dressier outfit. But don't fret! A simple chemise can be dressed up with a scarf and necklace. Pants and a blouse, or a two-piece dress in a silky fabric like polyester microfiber will be very lightweight and compact (see Tilley Endurables in Resources). A black rayon crepe split skirt and a blouse or a pastel chiffon-type skirt and a blouse make compact evening wear.

Respecting Local Customs

Research the areas you are going to visit. Consult your travel agent, guidebooks, and experienced travelers to find out about the standards of acceptable dress. In many foreign countries, modesty is the norm. Clothing should not be revealing in any way. Women should bring a scarf to cover the head and shoulders at religious sites. Avoid wearing shorts and low-cut blouses, skirts above the knee, and swimwear when you are away from the beach. If you must bring shorts, choose a baggy, knee-length style.

The climate of your destination can dictate your choice of color. Sunny places and informal cultures call for light, bright colors. In the large, older metropolitan areas of Europe and South America, tailored clothes in neutral and dark colors are more the norm. The color black is accepted as modern and sophisticated all year long in many large metropolitan cities in Europe, South America, and the United States. It may, however, look too somber in sunny Asian cities, the Mediterranean, and other coastal resort areas.

Clothing styles vary from city to city, even in the United States. Some countries require more formal dress; others are less restrictive. For example, in European cities, slacks are generally not worn by women to work or in dressy restaurants. Suit jackets are worn in offices, restaurants, and on the street. In India, a conservative suit would be inappropriate among the bright colored saris.

The safest strategy is to be tastefully dressed, perhaps on the conservative side. This means a jacket and tie (or a dark sweater and tie) for men, and a skirt and blouse or shirtwaist dress for women. For casual occasions, a button-down or polo-style shirt with short or long sleeves will always look appropriate. You can buy garments of the local style in the country you are visiting. In many countries, casual clothes such as jeans, jogging suits, athletic shoes, T-shirts, shorts, and resort wear will mark you as a tourist and should be reserved for the outdoors and resort areas.

In the Middle East and Asia, shoes are often removed in homes, temples, and mosques. Take shoes that are easy to put on and take off. (For visiting temples, tennis socks can be tucked in your daybag.) Observe your host and those around you to determine whether shoes are appropriate.

Bikinis are not acceptable at many destinations, and worn only by tourists in others. In resort areas that attract an international clientele, they are the norm. Ask your travel agent for advice and travel with a conservative one-piece suit unless you are sure a bikini is appropriate.

▼ Layering—Adjusting for Climate

The best approach is to pack thin layers of clothing that can be added or peeled off as the temperature changes. Avoid packing bulky sweaters and coats unless they are absolutely necessary. (If you need heavy items for only part of your trip, consider sending them home after you are finished using them.) The concept of layering is so important that I have organized all my travel wardrobes around it.

Layering means wearing several complementary lightweight garments rather than one or two bulky ones. Because different fabrics and fibers have different qualities, the layering pieces must be made in appropriate fibers, weights, and fabrics so that warmth, ventilation, and wind- and moisture-resistance will be provided without hindering your mobility.

There are four basic elements to the layering system: an underlayer, an insulating layer, an outer layer, and clothing for the extremities.

LAYER 1—THE UNDERLAYER

The first layer is worn against the skin and has two important functions. The first is to allow excess body heat to be released; for this, use a fabric that can breathe, such as a knit. The second is to carry (wick) perspiration away from the body. In warm weather, moisture should be absorbed by the fabric or wicked away, keeping the body dry. In cold weather, moisture should be transferred (wicked) away from the skin to the outer layers of the clothing, where it evaporates. Thus the body is kept warm and dry, even in wet weather.

Warm-weather underlayers — Knit T-shirts and tank tops are the perfect foundation for a layering system. In warm weather it might be your only layer. Cotton knit is comfortable, absorbs perspiration, and has a quick-cooling effect. However, in anything but hot and dry weather, it will get wet and stay wet. If you need fast-drying fabric, cotton/polyester knit is good. Rayon, cotton/polyester, and hydrophobic polyester knit T-shirts and tank tops, such as the Ray-T-ator by Sierra Designs, are available in outdoor stores and travel clothing catalogs (see Resources). These are highly packable and fast-drying, and they add a lot of versatility and performance to your wardrobe.

Choose a variety of styles to be dressed up or down. Polo-type shirts for men (to protect the neck from the sun) and jewelnecks for women are especially versatile.

Cotton-blend leggings and tights are excellent leg insulators. A pair of these with a big T-shirt will give you pajamas and lounge-wear, too.

For maximum travelability, choose moisture-wicking synthetic underwear, such as Capilene by Patagonia and Coolmax by Tarpon-wear. Otherwise, underpants should be of nylon or lightweight cotton in the smallest style you can wear.

Cold-weather underlayers — Packable, fast-drying, and hand wash-able, long underwear is one of the single most important investments you can make if you expect cold weather. It will keep you warm and dry on the coldest rainy nights, and keep the chill off during a brisk fall day so you don't need that bulky coat. In fact, it can prepare you for weather changes of up to 50 degrees. And as an added plus, it dou-bles as sleepwear so you don't have to pack pajamas. Used widely for outdoor clothing, modified polyester knits wick moisture away to the outer layers faster than natural fibers will. Polyester readily repels water, remains relatively warm when wet, and dries quickly. The new treated polyester knits, such as Capilene, Moisture Transfer System (MTS, made by REI), polypropylene, and Thermax, all have insulating prop-erties. Capilene, MTS, and Thermax are machine washable and dryable, and do not retain odors. Undershirts, pants, shorts, hats, socks, and gloves are all made from these comfortable materials. Remember that skin layers needn't look like long johns. Look for technical T-shirt and tank top styles by Sierra Designs and other outdoor manufactur-ers—these can double as long underwear.

Silk long underwear also provides lightweight, bulkless warmth. It is most suitable as a comfortable layer beneath street clothes. It is also great as sleepwear. The strong silk fibers retain body heat and the fabric can breathe. Available for men and women in all styles of shirts, camisoles, long underwear, briefs, and turtlenecks, silk underwear is hand washable and drip-dries quickly.

Silk underwear is available throughout the year from the mail-order companies Wintersilks and The Primary Layer. Seasonally it is available from the Eddie Bauer and Norm Thompson catalogs. Polyester-knit underwear is available year-round from mail-order catalogs, such as REI and Patagonia, and in outdoor stores. Seasonally it is also available from L. L. Bean and Land's End.

Use lightweight fabrics for highly aerobic activity, medium for stop-and-go and general travel, and heavy for extremely cold climates. If in doubt, it is best to err on the side of lightness; you can always adjust the outer layers for added warmth. Bring extra underwear for cold-weather destinations as it will dry more slowly. Nylon and silk dry faster than cotton. Note: Both silk and cotton lose their insulating abilities when wet.

LAYER 2—INSULATING LAYERS (REGULAR CLOTHING)

The insulating layers, in the form of shirts, slacks, sweaters, and jackets, are an integral part of the system. They trap air and keep the body warm, offer protection from sunburn, mosquitoes, etc., and should also wick moisture toward the outside. The particular garments you choose will depend on the weather.

Warm and hot weather — Shirts will be worn alone to ventilate the body, or layered over your T-shirt (which is Layer 1) to keep the chill off or protect you from mosquitoes and the sun. For maximum versatility, take loose-fitting, lightweight, button-down shirts and blouses made from cotton or cotton/polyester woven or knit fabrics. For wet or humid conditions, open-weave cotton or cotton mixed with Supplex nylon feels natural, is wrinkle-resistant, and dries quickly. Patagonia, TravelSmith, Norm Thompson, and L. L. Bean sell clothing that is ideal for casual or dressy situations in warm and tropical weather.

For men's dress shirts, the coarser weaves such as oxford cloth do better when packed in a carry-on. Finely woven cottons wrinkle very easily—forget them. Pack cotton and cotton/polyester blend shirts instead. (Land's End makes a cotton/polyester dress shirt.) For casual shirts, I recommend a wrinkle-resistant weave, such as chambray, twill, or seersucker, or a garment-washed fabric in a light to medium weight. Do not expect the pressed look unless you plan to bring an iron. Make sure to take a lightweight, long-sleeved shirt (and hat) for sun protection.

For warm weather, a thin cotton or cotton blend knit cardigan or pullover sweater is perfect. For women, cardigans are definitely the most versatile. They go with shorts, skirts, and slacks. If you expect temperatures to drop, take a cotton flannel or chamois-type shirt, a thin wool sweater, or a lightweight Polarfleece sweater, jacket, or vest. Fleece is just as warm as wool but is lighter, more compact, and dries quickly. Sierra Designs makes the lightweight Sierra fleece cardigan. Polarfleece is available under various brand names from L. L. Bean, REI, Patagonia, and other outdoor catalogs and retailers.

Jackets such as sport coats and blazers must be made of breathable, pliable, wrinkle-resistant fabric. Tropical- or medium-weight worsted or gabardine wool or wool blends, cotton and polyester blends, polyester microfiber, some silks, cotton, and linen-look blends are all recommended. Spandex is added to many fabrics now to improve their flexibility and comfort. Wrinkle-resistant travel jackets for men and women, available by mail order from Norm Thompson, include an eleven-pocket Frequent Flyer Jacket (65 percent polyester and 35 percent wool) and a seven-pocket Stretch Twill Travel Jacket (cotton and polyester). The Frequent Flyer comes in a four-pocket version for women. Patagonia offers a 100 percent microfiber jacket. TravelSmith, L. L. Bean, and Land's End also offer excellent sport coats for travel. These jackets typically come in khaki, navy, olive, and brown. Darker colors such as navy will give you maximum versatility for casual and dress wear. Jaeger and the above retailers also make fine women's blazers.

The world is increasingly informal and men can get by in many places without a sport coat. A dark pullover sweater, nice slacks, white shirt, and tie will do just fine. Jackets are, however, appropriate in cities for good restaurants and on cruises for the formal nights. Jackets are essential if you are doing any kind of business. In many parts of the world, they are necessary unless you are on a casual trip. Ask your travel agent or host for advice. If you do take one, try "the uniform"— navy blazer, gray and/or tan slacks, white shirt, burgundy sweater, tie. This look is appropriate for any occasion.

Women can base their entire wardrobe around the versatile two-piece dress. In a fabric that is suitable for day or evening, such as a knit or a rayon crepe, the matching skirt and top will give you lots of clothing options. Worn as a dress, the outfit can be formal enough for the theater or dinner; worn separately, the pieces can be mixed and matched with other pieces. If the top is a button-down style with a straight finished bottom, it can be tucked in or worn out, or layered over other tops as a light jacket. A two-piece dress is far easier to pack than a one-piece dress is.

If you must take a dress, look for a neutral, chemise-style dress in a cotton or wool knit that can be transformed easily for day and evening. For warm weather, a cotton shirtwaist dress is useful.

Slacks, skirts, and shorts should be made of cotton, cotton/polyester, or lightweight wool. Some synthetics work well too. Spandex makes clothing comfortable even on long plane rides. Roomy pants and shorts are available in Supplex nylon, which is compact, light, and cool. An extremely wind-resistant fabric, it dries quickly in hot weather, making it ideal for beach, desert, boat, and other warm weather vacations. Being compact, it is also a good choice for athletic suits, as is polyester microfiber. Slacks should be loose fitting for ventilation and should not chafe.

People love denim jeans, and they are worn all over the world. They are sturdy and very forgiving in the soil and stain departments, making them perfect travel garments for parents with small children, for some casual travelers, or for "dress-down" days in general.

However, jeans are limited as a travel garment when you don't have room to bring a lot of clothes. They don't transition from day into evening, or from casual to dressy occasions. Also, they are bulky, difficult to hand wash, and slow to dry. Finally, if jeans become wet, they stay wet—and cold, too.

Jeans are at their best in moderate temperatures, that is, when it's not too hot, cold, or wet. To be a good travel garment, they should be soft, lightweight, loose fitting, and non-chafing. A washer and dryer should be accessible. Otherwise, stick to fabrics such as cotton twill, cotton/polyester, supplex nylon, and linen, or Travelsmith's Tencel denim (available in pants, skirts, vest, and a dress).

Skirts should have pockets and be simply styled (one should be mid-length). They should also be loose fitting and allow the use of a security wallet. I also like skorts or culottes, especially for cruises.

Shorts should be knee-length with lots of pockets. Supplex nylon shorts will double for swim trunks and casual wear; look for the longer versions.

Temperate to cold weather — In cool to cold weather, choose jackets, slacks, and skirts in light- or medium-weight wool and wool blends, heavier cotton and cotton blends, and polyester microfiber. Wool knits, especially merino wool, are excellent for dresses and women's coordinates. They're comfortable enough to sleep in. Sweaters and cardigans should be made of finely knit wool such as cashmere or merino. Or, for casual and active trips, include a lighter-weight polyester fleece jacket or vest for excellent breathability, warmth, and fast-drying properties. Blouses can be cotton, cotton/polyester, or silk-like synthetics, including polyester. Men (and women) should take travel-worthy, cotton/polyester, long-sleeved oxfords or pinpoints (available from Land's End for men and women). Add layering pieces such as a knit turtleneck or jewelneck, and long-sleeved shirts of cotton knit, chamois, wool flannel, or 100 weight fleece.

LAYER 3—OUTERWEAR/RAINGEAR

For the general traveler, this top layer will protect against rain, wind, and moisture while allowing body heat to escape. If you choose to bring your London Fog raincoat, keep in mind that it will have to be worn or carried on your arm. Better to choose a coat that is water-repellent (as opposed to water*proof*), breathable, and packable. Your style, destinations, and activities will dictate its form. A full-length microfiber raincoat or a coated nylon taffeta version of this is perfect for city sightseeing and evenings at the theater; a nylon anorak is great for casual travel, beach trips, or warm/cool weather trips. To make these coats water-repellent, you can buy Kenyon Water Repellency, a liquid that you add to the wash cycle. Or you can spray with Scotchguard. Follow care instructions for your garment in all cases. Packing a small umbrella is must.

For more extreme conditions or for "singing in the rain," you may need to substitute or add a layer that is water*proof* and breathable. A rain jacket and rain pants or a waterproof poncho is a must for avid walkers and hikers. These garments, usually bulkier than their repellent counterparts, are made from highly technical, laminated fabrications (the most famous of which is Gore-Tex) and can be found at outdoor stores by manufacturers such as REI, Sierra Designs, and Patagonia.

I don't recommend plastic unless it is for back-up use only. Plastic is bulky, heavy, doesn't breathe, and is difficult to reuse.

LAYER 4—THE EXTREMITIES

You can be pretty miserable if your limbs are cold and wet. These are the necessities to protect your head, hands, and feet. Bring a hat for rain and/or shine. There are myriad hats on the market. Look for one that is wide brimmed, packable, breathable, and suitable to your activities. "Baseball" type hats should have a large bill. A dark underside absorbs UV rays. Chin straps or a cinch strap around the head are desirable for windy weather. If you need your hat to float, look for a closed-cell foam layer in the top. To protect your neck from the hot sun, some models, such as the Supplex nylon Skyline Packhat, feature a hanging fabric drape to cover your neck and ears.

Sun hats are made of cotton, wool, felt, hemp, Supplex nylon, or grass (Panama hats). Supplex nylon dries fast and protects you from UV rays, as do Solumbra hats (SPF 30).

Rain or shine hats are usually made of cotton duck, wool felt, coated Supplex nylon, or waxed cotton. Among many excellent hat manufacturers are Tilley, Ultimate, Watership Trading Company, and Lights of the Sky, Ltd.

Balaclavas, headguards, and headbands for ear covering should all be considered for cold weather.

To protect your hands from cold and wet, consider modified polyester (i.e., Capilene) or silk knit glove liners.

Socks should be in thin and medium weights that can be layered and will dry quickly. Buy socks that will wick moisture away from the foot (typically cotton/synthetic blends). All-cotton socks are comfortable in very hot weather, but when they get wet, they stay wet and lose their insulating ability. If you like all-cotton socks, bring extras. Choose socks that match your activities. Thorlo makes socks for every imaginable activity, featuring extra cushioning in critical areas. For a little extra warmth and comfort, consider fleece socks (which double as slippers) and silk or modified polyester knit sock liners.

Tights instead of hose keep you warm in cold weather.

You may want to invest in a lightweight, packable pair of galoshes to cover your shoes for rain, or, before you go, treat your shoes with water repellent to protect them.

▼ Clothing Care on the Road

Plan on doing a little laundry every night or every other night instead of saving it all up. I wash underwear in the shower at night, hang them to dry, and they're ready by morning. This way, you'll need to take fewer clothes.

Check all garment labels for specific care requirements. Be sure to choose fabrics that are easily washed on the road. Always use a gentle soap (never harsh detergents) for washing. Clothes-washing items you might want to bring are listed on pp. 218–219.

HANDWASHING COTTON, SILK, AND DELICATES

1. Fill the sink or tub with lukewarm water. Add travel soap or a cold-water detergent, such as Woolite.
2. Swish the garment (do not squeeze, twist, or rub it) for a couple of minutes.
3. Rinse thoroughly in cold water.
4. Lay the wet garment on a towel (a Packtowl is ideal for this) and roll it up to remove excess water.
5. Hang cotton, synthetics, and natural and synthetic blends to dry. Iron cottons with moderate to high heat, synthetics and blends with low heat.

Woven silk should be ironed, dry or with steam, *while still wet*, until the garment is dry. Use a press cloth. To avoid wrinkles, wash only what you have time to press immediately. It is hard to get wrinkles out after clothes have dried.

HANDWASHING WOOL AND OTHER SWEATERS

Caution: Wool takes time to dry except in very hot, dry weather.

1. Fill the sink with cool or cold water. Add a cold-water detergent such as Woolite.

2. Soak garment for three minutes.

3. Squeeze soapy water very gently through the sweater.

4. Rinse thoroughly in cool or cold water.

5. Roll the sweater in a Packtowl or ordinary towel to remove excess moisture. Do not wring or twist.

6. Dry the sweater flat. Block it to the original size if needed.

REMOVING WRINKLES

Hang out tomorrow's outfit to get the closet wrinkles out. Remember to take an extension cord and adapter plugs to use with your iron (and a converter if it is not dual-voltage). Be sure the garments are cool and dry before wearing them. If they are still warm, the pressing will fall out.

Ironing — Use an iron to add crispness to a garment (especially with cotton or linen) and to press creases in.

1. Turn down the bedcovers to create an ironing surface.

2. Test the iron heat on an underside, hidden edge of the fabric first. Synthetics take low heat; natural fibers take higher heat.

3. Press garments on the wrong side with a press cloth to prevent shine or scorch. (A large handkerchief or a used sheet of fabric-softener works as a press cloth and allows you to see what you are doing.)

4. If desired, use spray starch to keep cotton looking crisp.

5. Do not move or wear garment until it is completely cool.

Steam-and-dry — This method makes wrinkles fall out of dry clothes.

1. Hang one or a few sets of clothes in the bathroom.

2. Turn on the hot water in the shower or bathtub.

3. Wet your hand and glide it vertically down the garment, moistening the fabric.

4. When the shower is steaming or the tub is between one-third and half full, turn off the water and close the door.

5. Leave the clothes hanging up for thirty minutes or up to two hours, depending on the fabrics. Wools, wool blends, and most synthetic blends steam out well, as do most linen and cotton blends. Silks and cottons should not be left to steam, because they are so absorbent.

6. Let clothes air dry before wearing them.

Travel steamer — Use a steamer to remove travel wrinkles and creases. Steamers are lighter than irons and may be used anywhere in the room where you can hang a garment—you need not create an ironing surface. They work best on light and medium fabrics but cannot be used to press a garment.

1. Hang up garment from a door or window rod.

2. Fill the steamer as indicated, and wait about five minutes for steam to develop. (You can add a pinch of salt to hasten the process.)

3. Glide the steaming head along the garment, pulling and smoothing the fabric with the other hand as you go. Wrinkles should fall out easily.

4. Make sure that you empty, rinse, and dry the steamer after each use, according to instructions.

Quick method — Wrinkle-Free is a commercial fabric-relaxer spray that can be found in drugstores, travel stores, and luggage shops. It can remove wrinkles from almost all fabrics, except for 100 percent polyester. It is a spot treatment and works best on absorbent fabrics such as cotton, wool, and silk. To use, spray the garment, smoothing out the wrinkles by hand.

STAIN REMOVAL

Part of maintaining your clothes on the road is dealing with the inevitable stains acquired while picnicking, in restaurants, and in general activity. The best guide on the subject is Don Aslett's *Stain Buster's Bible: The Complete Guide to Stain Removal* (NAL-Dutton, 1990). If you prefer to use natural ingredients, read *Clean & Green: The Complete Guide to Nontoxic and Environmentally Safe Housekeeping* by Annie Berthold-Bond (Ceres Press, 1990).

Before you start trying to remove a stain, make sure you know what kind of fabric you are working with and what caused the stain. Check the clothing tag; some stain-removal agents should not be used on certain fabrics. General procedures:

▼ Treat stains *immediately, before they set*. Sponge or rinse with cool water or club soda. Fresh stains are much easier to remove.

▼ Take dry-cleanables in immediately for professional treatment if possible.

▼ Do *not* apply heat from hot water, an iron, or a dryer until stain is removed. Heat will set most stains. Start with cold water, then go on to warm.

▼ Test the garment for colorfastness by using the agent first on a hidden inside seam or the hem. Bleach and ammonia should be diluted before being used at all.

▼ First blot, absorb, or scrape off all excess liquid or solids, thus removing much of the potential stain.

▼ Remove stains by blotting, flushing (applying liquid so it flows through the fabric), or rinsing, not by rubbing.

▼ Apply stain removers and rinsing liquid to the back of the stain. When applying always work from the *outside in* to contain the stain.

▼ Rinsing a dry-cleanable item means sponge-rinsing with a wet clean cloth. Put a dry cloth on the opposite side to absorb excess water as you rinse. Never flush a dry-cleanable garment.

▼ Avoid leaving a ring by "feathering" or blending the edges of the wet spot into the dry area after each rinse. Lightly wipe off with a lifting motion from the inside out.

▼ Shoes

The quest for comfortable travel shoes should equal your determination to travel light. Comfort has to be the top priority when you are purchasing shoes. Luckily several manufacturers make wonderful-looking men's and women's shoes that combine good looks with comfort. Try to limit yourself to three pairs of shoes. I suggest bringing a formal shoe, walking shoe, and sandals or thongs. In all cases, search for versatile, multipurpose styles. For example, Rockport makes DresSport shoes that are appropriate for all but the most formal occasions. Teva or Clark sandals are also good walking shoes. Ecco Mobiles can be worn hiking and in the city, too. Other quality brands are Merrill, Timberland, SAS, and Easy Spirit.

Recommendations

The Walk Shop in Berkeley, California, which specializes in comfortable shoes, has a number of recommendations:

▼ All shoes should have springy, resilient composition soles that cushion the step as you walk. Leather is usually too hard. Injection-molded soles form a permanent unit and are highly recommended.

▼ Look for thick or Vibram soles.

▼ Buy a shoe with an adjustable lace or strap because your foot changes size during the day. Slip-ons are better for short-term, rather than long-term, comfort.

▼ For tropical weather, look for open styles that allow your feet to breathe.

▼ Some shoes, such as those made by Mephisto, Clark's, and Ecco, have "air-conditioning," sophisticated airflow systems built into the sole to ventilate the foot.

▼ Some people need or wish to let their shoes dry completely between wearings. If you do, take an extra pair of shoes, or buy shoes, such as those made by Ecco or Rockport, that come with removable insoles that can be taken out and dried between wearings. Instead of alternating shoes, you can just change the insoles. Or buy Spenco removable insoles. For excessive perspiration, look for a lined shoe.

▼ Definitely take a pair of sandals for warm weather. Highly recommended are the three-strap, orthopedic-footbed sandal made by Clark's for women, or the Teva for men and women. These double as walking shoes. For men and women, Reiker makes a design that is part shoe and part sandal, with a T-strap.

- Make sure your shoes are big enough and fit property. Try them on with the socks you intend to wear. Pay attention to the fit more than to the size.

- Make sure that you wear your shoes at least six or even twelve times before your trip. This gives you time to make necessary adjustments before you leave.

- Consider water repellency. Many types of walking shoes are now made with waterproof leather. If you need to treat your shoes, get an alcohol-based treatment (not a silicone-based one) for general travel, such as Water Repellent Shield, an aerosol by Cadillac. Silicone-based treatments seal the shoe completely and are recommended for hiking boots. Ultra Seal Waterproofing Boot Treatment Creme or Ultrathon Spray Boot Protection, both available at REI, are silicone-based. Both will darken the leather slightly as they provide protection against rain.

▼ Accessories

Accessories greatly expand the versatility of your travel wardrobe, enabling you to make a simple day outfit into dramatic evening attire. The travel wardrobe is a simple, classic background—accessories will add variety, texture, and color. They take up little room and will be a cheerful addition to your wardrobe.

SCARVES

- 1 large (at least 35 inches) square shawl. This is the most versatile shape and can be used to dress up a jacket, dress, or blouse. A shawl can be used as a head covering for religious sites, as an emergency blanket, and, in warm weather, will protect you from the sun or take the chill off in air-conditioned rooms.

- 1 long rectangle. Use it as a sash or with a blouse.

- 1 square (at least 25 inches square). A large bandanna is a good all-purpose scarf.

BELTS

Take one or two in leather or fabric in neutral colors, or take high-quality elasticized belts with one or two interchangeable buckles. A snazzy metallic belt is useful for eveningwear. Covered buckles will match jewelry of any color. Fabric belts are appropriate for casual garments and warm climates. Some belts have zippers in the back to hide money.

JEWELRY

Keep it simple! Gold is universally appropriate, as are pearls for dressing up. Choose a few basic pieces: one pair of earrings that can be slept in, one pair of evening earrings, costume pearls, and a simple gold chain. But if you love jewelry, here is where you can splurge. Do not take anything of monetary or sentimental value. It is not worth risking the loss. If you do decide to bring valuables, carry them in your security wallet and deposit them in the hotel's safe deposit box. (Also see chapter 10 on security; not all hotels are trustworthy.)

SHOE CLIPS

Found in shoe departments, these clip-on decorations dress up pumps. You can also use clip-on earrings for this purpose.

HOSE

Plain stockings are the norm for business, but you can use color and texture to spice up your outfits for casual or evening wear. If you wear anything other than regular sizes, plan on taking enough hose from home to cover your trip. Take clear nail polish to stop runs. Also, try pre-washing your nylons—they won't run as quickly as new ones!

PURSES/FANNY PACKS

Take one *small*, packable purse with a long shoulder strap. Select a simple and slightly elegant style that is also appropriate for a dressy evening. This is for your comb, tissues, pen, glasses, and a few dollars. You may also want to wear a fanny pack on a casual trip. For better security, get one that you can thread through your belt loops.

Important: Neither your purse nor your fanny pack should hold more than basic necessities such as notebook, pen, glasses, Kleenex,

Chapstick, medications, and the like. A small amount of cash for the next few hours is all the money that you need. *All* your other valuables should *always* remain in your money belt.

▼ Making Your Packing List—Three Steps to Avoid "Just-in-Case" Syndrome

Make a packing list—it is very important. To avoid over- or underpacking, take the following three steps to focus on your wardrobe and travel-gear requirements for your trip. (Also see chapter 1, Planning in a Nutshell.)

Step 1. Research the Weather

Use your travel itinerary, weather information from CNN, the Weather Channel, the Web, the newspaper, or an almanac such as the *International Traveler's Weather Guide* by Tom Loffman (see Resources p. 202), and the Itinerary Wardrobe Planner (see pp. 94–95) to predict the temperature range and rain and humidity levels for your destinations. This will help you decide how many layers to bring and what types and weights of fabrics you will need. Pinpointing lodging and laundry facilities will clue you in to what fabrics will be maintainable and how many items of clothing you will need, given your laundry schedule (i.e., staying at a bed-and-breakfast on a Sunday means you'll have to handwash, but London on a Monday means you'll be able to send out dry cleaning).

Step 2. Analyze Your Activities

Use the Daily Activity Planner on p. 96 to list clothing and gear needed each day for special events, sightseeing, outdoor and sports activities, and business meetings. Figure out in advance how you will create outfits for any special situations. Then use this information to complete your packing list.

Step 3. Make Your Packing List

Fill out the Women's Packing List on p. 97 or Men's Packing List on p. 98. Circle wardrobe items you need, then use this as a shopping list for any pieces needed to complete your wardrobe. When you pack the item, check it off. If it doesn't all fit in your suitcase, adjust your wardrobe and redo your list. Immediately after your trip, review the list and, for future reference, cross out items you didn't need. You can also use it as an inventory for insurance purposes should your belongings get lost. Whenever possible, keep shopping receipts for this purpose. If you travel frequently, you might develop a "business trip" list, a "vacation" list, a "weekend" list, etc. Keep these on your computer or in your suitcase.

▼ Itinerary Wardrobe Planner

Day No.	Date	Day of the week	Destination and type of lodging
1			
2			
3			
4			
5			
6			
7			
8			
9			
10			
11			
12			
13			
14			
15			
16			
17			
18			
19			
20			
21			
22			
23			
24			
25			
26			
27			
28			
29			
30			
31			

Weather Forecast				
High	Low	Rain	Humidity	Laundry facilities

▼ Daily Activity Planner

Day No.	Date		Location	
	Morning Activities	**Afternoon Activities**	**Evening Activities**	**Other Activities**
Layer 1 Underlayer				
Layer 2 Clothing				
Layer 3 Outerlayer				
Layer 4 Extremities; Shoes				
Accessories				
Gear				

▼ Women's Packing List

▼ Underlayer
- ☐ thermal underwear
- ☐ underpants
- ☐ bras
- ☐ garment shields
- ☐ hose, day
- ☐ hose, eve
- ☐ leggings/tights
- ☐ nightgown/big T-shirt
- ☐ swimsuit
- ☐ active wear
- ☐ pareo/sarong

▼ Clothing
- ☐ jacket #1
- ☐ jacket #2
- ☐ skirt #1
- ☐ skirt #2
- ☐ pants #1
- ☐ pants #2
- ☐ two-piece dress
- ☐ dress
- ☐ cardigan/sweater
- ☐ long-sleeved shirt
- ☐ shirt #2
- ☐ shirt #3
- ☐ shirt #4
- ☐ T-shirts
- ☐ shorts
- ☐ athletic, sport clothing
- ☐ other _____

▼ Outerlayer
- ☐ raincoat
- ☐ parka
- ☐ rainjacket
- ☐ rainpants
- ☐ windbreaker
- ☐ poncho
- ☐ umbrella

▼ Extremities
- ☐ shoes, dress
- ☐ shoes, walking
- ☐ sandals
- ☐ slippers
- ☐ socks, dress
- ☐ socks, casual
- ☐ sun hat
- ☐ rain hat
- ☐ ear warmers
- ☐ gloves/liners
- ☐ sock liners

▼ Accessories
- ☐ belts, day
- ☐ belts, evening
- ☐ bandanna
- ☐ scarves
- ☐ handbag
- ☐ necklace
- ☐ pin
- ☐ earrings
- ☐ bracelets
- ☐ watch

▼ Men's Packing List

▼ Underlayer

- ☐ thermal underwear
- ☐ underpants
- ☐ undershirts
- ☐ big T-shirt
- ☐ pajamas
- ☐ swim trunks
- ☐ active wear
- ☐ pareo/sarong

▼ Clothing

- ☐ jacket #1
- ☐ jacket #2
- ☐ slacks #1
- ☐ slacks #2
- ☐ slacks #3
- ☐ vest
- ☐ sweater
- ☐ fleece jacket
- ☐ long-sleeved shirt
- ☐ shirt #1
- ☐ shirt #2
- ☐ shirt #3
- ☐ shirt #4
- ☐ T-shirts
- ☐ shorts
- ☐ athletic, sport clothing
- ☐ other _____

▼ Outerlayer

- ☐ raincoat
- ☐ parka
- ☐ rainjacket
- ☐ rainpants
- ☐ windbreaker
- ☐ poncho
- ☐ umbrella

▼ Extremities

- ☐ shoes, dress
- ☐ shoes, walking
- ☐ sandals
- ☐ slippers
- ☐ socks, dress
- ☐ socks, casual
- ☐ sun hat
- ☐ rain hat
- ☐ ear warmers
- ☐ gloves/liners
- ☐ sock liners

▼ Accessories

- ☐ belts, day
- ☐ belts, evening
- ☐ bandanna
- ☐ ties
- ☐ watch
- ☐ cufflinks

▼ Tips to Lighten the Load

These are tried-and-true tips from my audience!

- ▼ Wear your heaviest or bulkiest clothes and shoes on the plane.
- ▼ Take old underwear and socks and discard them as you go.
- ▼ Wear old walking shoes and discard them on the last day of your trip.
- ▼ Pack old clothes and give them away or discard them as you go to make room for souvenirs and new purchases.
- ▼ Don't pack too many T-shirts—buy them along the way.
- ▼ Sell your jeans.
- ▼ Leave appliances at home.
- ▼ Send off or give away paper materials as you go—paper is heavy.
- ▼ Carry small bottles of toiletries.
- ▼ Remove all excess packaging.
- ▼ As a last resort, and to concentrate on your resolve, pack your bag and walk a mile carrying it. If you can handle it, well and good; if it is too heavy, be ruthless.

▼ Traveling to Opposite Climates

If it's winter here, chances are you are headed for warmer weather. Or vice versa! What should you wear on the plane? In all cases, try and choose versatile, seasonless fabrics such as light-or medium-weight wool, synthetics, and cotton polyester.

Travel from warm to cold weather:

- ▼ Pick as compact a version of a coat as you can, such as a microfiber raincoat with zip-out lining or a thin-but-warm cashmere coat. Select boots that are pliable and can be packed easily.

- ▼ Try shipping your coat and boots ahead. Write on the package "hold for" with your name and arrival date. Have the hotel hold it for you until you arrive. This also works if the first part of your trip is warm and the second part is cold.

▼ Carry your coat on your arm or in your extra folding nylon bag. Wear your boots on the plane.

▼ The last resort—size up to a 24-or 26-inch suitcase or a garment bag and pack your coat and boots. Check your bag.

▼ If the weather warms up mid-trip, ship your coat and boots home.

If you are traveling from cold to warm weather:

▼ At the airport store your coat in a locker or leave it in the car trunk.

▼ Plan to wear a few items that will be worn specifically for the cold part of the journey. To the plane, wear long underwear, a warm top, hat, gloves, sock liners, and a scarf. Wear your arrival travel clothing, whatever that might be, with a sweater. On the plane or at the airport you can pack these compact items away into your luggage, and you'll be ready for arrival.

5

How to Pack Your Suitcase

In this chapter, I will show you how to pack each of the basic carry-on pieces using the Bundle Method. *Once you know how to make "the bundle," you can apply it to any 21- or 22-inch carry-on, or 24-inch checkable pullman.* (The 20-inch also works if you are small or plan to bring minimal clothing.) This includes one-compartment suitcases, such as wheelaboards and wheelaboards with "suiter" options; two-compartment pullmans; three-compartment (3-zip) shoulder bags; and the convertible backpack. (Used for a travel pack, the method may need to be modified to accommodate the body's center of gravity if you will be walking extensively.)

For those of you who require business or larger wardrobes, or simply more room for gear, I have added instructions for packing a carry-on with folded shirts, packing a garment bag, and packing larger, 26-inch and 29-inch (checkable) standard pullmans. Included also are tips for packing your secondary tote or daypack and a duffel bag.

Important: Do *not* pack valuables such as passport, cash, credit cards, traveler's checks, tickets, extra photos, documents, and prescriptions. These go, *not* in your purse, your fanny pack, your carry-on, your briefcase, or any other piece of luggage, but *on your person*, under your clothes, in a security wallet. No ifs, ands, or buts about it. (See pp. 36–39.)

▼ The Bundle Method

The Bundle Method is a packing system perfect for soft-sided luggage. It creates a cushioned, woven mass of clothing (the bundle) that does not shift and hardly wrinkles. It is more versatile than rolling or folding because it accommodates tailored clothing, such as skirts, slacks, and shirts or blouses, as well as the more casual T-shirts and jeans.

Two key features make the bundle an asset for any traveler. First, it is a single unit of clothing that takes up the entire space in a 21- or 22-inch-long carry-on or a 24-inch checkable bag. In a completely filled case clothes move around less and are less likely to wrinkle. Second, the bundle has no sharp folds or creases, only soft, cushioned edges. The bundle is made up of layers of clothing wrapped around an inner cushion I call the core, which is a pouch containing lingerie, underwear, socks, and other accessories. Each item of clothing is cushioned; because there are no sharp creases, the clothes virtually do not wrinkle.

Before we pack anything, let's look at the bundle as it would appear after you have finished packing.

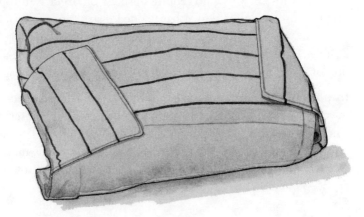

The bundle.

Packing It All In

The bundle contains wardrobe items only. We will deal with travel gear later. Do not start packing until you have assembled every last item. Then read the directions for packing, right through, beginning with the next paragraph. There's more to packing than dumping stuff in a case and hoping you can shut the lid—but then you knew that, or you wouldn't be reading this book. I'll start with some general tips and then go on with detailed instructions for packing the different items of clothing.

Always start with the largest, heaviest, and longest items of clothing, typically a jacket or straight dress, but not slacks. First pack tailored clothing that is likely to wrinkle. Save knits and wrinkle-resistant items for later.

Align collars and waistbands flat along the edge of the bag, not pushed up against the sides.

The sequence of what goes in first varies for each person according to the size of the garments. Generally, large jackets and sweaters go in first, followed by smaller garments. This is because they will have more room to wrap around the core. Experiment with your clothes to find your appropriate packing sequence.

The Bundle Method does not require covering garments with plastic. However, if you have delicate fabrics which wrinkle easily, you can encase the garment in a plastic dry cleaning bag. I usually use plastic only for hanging items in suiters or garment bags. For more on the use of plastic, see the discussions of the various packing methods that follow in this chapter, and pp. 205–206.

Tissue paper can be rolled and stuffed in sleeves and under collars to decrease wrinkling.

Getting Started

Before you begin, clear a large space for packing, such as your bed or a large table. A clothing rack is a spacesaver for hanging wardrobe items instead of stacking them.

Gather the following packing aids: core pouch (see p. 111), shoe covers, a plastic dry cleaning bag if you are hanging a suit in a wheel-aboard "suiter," and tissue paper if desired.

1. Put aside those clothes you will wear on the plane.

2. Make another pile of clothing and accessories you will want quick access to on arrival—for example, a big T-shirt, nightwear, workout clothes or swimsuit, shorts and a T-shirt, or a rainjacket. These are your "accessibles."

3. Gather your shoes. Stuff them with rolled-up socks, hose, and underwear. Place in shoe covers or plastic bags (do not seal). Tip: A woman's shoes can often be packed inside a man's pair to save space.

4. Gather belts, ties (with or without tie case), and scarves.

5. Gather underwear, socks, hose, and other *wardrobe*-related accessories and place them in your core pouch.

6. Have your travel kits on hand, packed in nylon pouches or plastic Ziploc bags. Also include hat, travel raincoat and umbrella, small purse, and appliances. We will get to these after we make the bundle.

7. Stack the rest of your wardrobe on the bed or hang it on a clothes rack. Button shirts and zip zippers. If you are using a hanging clothes caddy, hang the garments as they are listed, from left to right; if you are using your bed, stack them from the bottom of the list up, so that item number one is on top. Arrange as applicable:

WOMEN

1. Long *straight* skirt or *straight* dress
2. Jacket
3. Straight skirts
4. Dress—A-line or full-skirted
5. Skirt—A-line or full-skirted
6. Slacks or split skirts

7. Shirts, long-sleeved (with scarf, if any)

8. Shirts, short-sleeved (with scarf, if any)

9. Sweater or other knits (if any)

10. Shorts

MEN

1. Jacket

2. Slacks

3. Shirts, long-sleeved

4. Shirts, short-sleeved

5. Sweater or other knits

6. Shorts

MAKING THE BUNDLE

Lay the suitcase on the bed. Open the deepest section completely so that the bag lies flat.

Pretend the base of your open suitcase is a clockface. Garments will be the "hands" of the clock—placed alternately in 12 o'clock, 3 o'clock, 6 o'clock, and 9 o'clock directions. We will be using the vertical (12 o'clock and 6 o'clock) dimensions of the case for jackets, shirts, straight dresses, and skirts. The horizontal (9 o'clock and 3 o'clock) dimensions will be used for slacks, tri-folded items (full dresses and skirts, A-line skirts), and other narrow items like sashes.

Note: The "hinge end" is the wall of the bag that will touch the floor when the bag is put down. The "top end" is opposite from the hinge end, where the handle is.

Straight dress or straight long skirt — (Illustration A.) For a straight dress, place the shoulders in the corners. Center the collar at the hinge end of the case so that the shoulders of the dress remain smooth. Make sure that the dress collar meets but does not bend against the wall of the bag.

Now, drape the bottom of the dress over the opposite end of the bag (where the handle is). Drape the sleeves, if any, over the side

A. Straight dresses or straight
   long skirts, if any, go in first.
   Otherwise start with your jacket.

B. Jacket is laid face up, with
   centered collar flat, sleeves
   and hem draped (Method 1).
   See also Method 2, p. 107.

C. Full skirts are folded lengthwise
   and packed horizontally. Place
   hem first, draping the waistband.

walls of the bag. Smooth out the dress along the floor of the bag as best you can.

Jacket — This will make your first layer if you do not have a straight dress or long straight skirt. There are two ways to pack it:

Method 1: (Illustration B.) Button the jacket and lay it in the suitcase face up. The collar should lie flat, flush with, but not bending up against, the hinge end of the case, to allow the width of the collar and shoulders to remain smooth. Center the collar and hold it down using one hand. With the other hand, drape the bottom of the jacket over the handle (top) end of the bag. Drape the sleeves over the short sides of the bag. Use all of the space in the bag; get as close to the walls of the bag as possible.

Method 2: If the jacket is too wide or the sleeves do not drape easily, unbutton the jacket and lay it in the suitcase face down, with the collar flat. Bring in the lapels so that the width of the jacket fits the bag. Drape the bottom of the jacket over the handle (top) end of the bag. Bring the sleeves into the bag, laying them vertically down the jacket. Cushion the crease in the shoulder area if you wish. The fold will fall out quickly when the jacket is worn.

Straight skirts — Lay the skirt on top of the jacket, with the waistband at the *opposite* edge of the case from the jacket collar. Hold down the skirt with one hand and smooth it out with the other. Drape the bottom of the skirt over the opposite end of the bag. Add another skirt if desired, alternating waistbands.

A-line or full-skirted dress — Remember, full skirts and dresses are not recommended. If you must take one, you will have to fold it in thirds (tri-fold) before packing it. Lay the dress face down on a flat surface. Fold one side in, forming a straight vertical line. Fold the sleeve down vertically. Repeat for the other side. Now lay the dress in the bag horizontally, with the middle portion lying along the floor of the bag. Drape the shoulders over one side and the hem over the other.

A-line or full skirts — (Illustration C.) These, too, you will have to tri-fold lengthwise and pack using the horizontal direction of the bag. Lay the skirt on the bed. Fold in one side, a third, forming a straight vertical fold. Repeat on the opposite side. If you would like to cushion

D. Slacks are packed horizontally. Match
the creases and place the waistband
along the edge, then smooth and drape.

E. Long-sleeved shirts are next (Method 1).
Collars are face up; sleeves and hem are
draped. See also Method 2.

F. Short-sleeved shirts, T-shirts, and knits are
next. Shorts and swimsuits are last. The core
containing underwear is placed in the center.

these folds, place some nylons, socks, or tissue paper in them to minimize the crease. Now, using the horizontal direction, lay the hem at one edge of the bag. Smooth the skirt, and drape the waistband over the opposite side. (Hems will wrinkle less if packed this way.)

Slacks — (Illustration D.) Match up the creases in both legs. Lay the slacks over the jacket (or skirts), bringing the waistband flush with the bag's narrow side. Smooth out the slacks and drape the bottoms over the opposite wall. If you have another pair, repeat the exercise, this time placing the waistband against the opposite edge.

Long-sleeved shirts — (Illustration E.) *Method 1.* Lay shirts or blouses faceup in the bag as you did the jacket, making sure to alternate collars. Make sure the collars are flat and not pushing up against the side of the bag. Drape the sleeves and bottoms over the sides.

Method 2. If your shirt is wider than the suitcase, use the face-down method. Lay the shirt face down, with the collar centered. Vertically fold each side of the shirt so that the edges align with the side of the bag. Cross the sleeves over the back of the shirt. If needed, fold the sleeve ends across the side of the shirt. Drape the bottom. (If you prefer to pack folded shirts, see "How to Pack Folded Shirts," pp. 118–119.)

Scarves — If you have scarves, pack them as a layer next to the blouse you might be wearing. (Similarly, once you are familiar with the technique, try putting whole outfits together.)

Short-sleeved shirts – (Illustration F.) Place them in the same way that you placed long-sleeved shirts. Lay them in the case, center the collar, and drape the bottom and sides over the walls of the case.

Now you are finished with all of the wrinkle-prone, tailored items. You have also reached the center of the bundle. Here is where you put knits such as sweaters.

Sweater — Place your sweater or other knits over the blouses. Drape the bottom and sides.

Shorts — Where you place shorts depends upon their length. Match up the seams. For long shorts, use the vertical direction of the bag, adding them soon after the slacks. For short shorts, use the horizontal direction, adding them last.

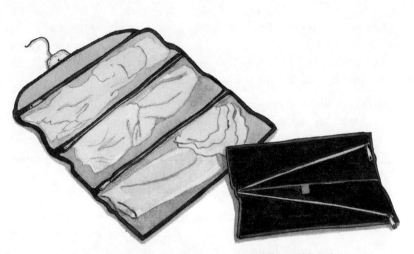

G. Samples of core pouches: these go in the middle of
your clothing bundle. For the organizer on the left,
tuck in hanger and fold pouch in half before packing.

H. Close the bundle by folding in sleeves and hems.
By smoothing as you go and packing tightly,
you will end up with fewer wrinkles in your clothes.

Undershirts, boxer shorts, and sleepwear — These can be folded neatly and placed in the center of the space. Or place your sleepwear on top of the finished bundle so that it will be accessible upon arrival.

THE CORE POUCH

The core — (Illustration G.) The core acts as the center cushion, supporting the layers of clothing you have just put in. It is made up of a pouch (about 11 × 16 inches) containing your swimsuit and other wardrobe accessories such as lingerie, undergarments, socks, belt buckles, and so on. I recommend the Carry-rite Mini-organizer (#215) and the Deluxe Core Pouch (available at Easy Going—see Resources). Do not use a plastic resealable bag for the core: It is slippery and will cause garments to shift.

Place the core in the center of the bag with about 2 inches of space all around it. (Illustration F.) Make sure that the edges are nice and full—the better the edges are built up, the less wrinkling. If you don't have a core pouch, simply place the items in the middle to fill an 11 × 16-inch space.

TO CLOSE THE BUNDLE

The core will be covered by layers of the clothing that you draped over the sides of the bag. Fold back the bottom of the garment that was layered immediately below the core. (Illustration H.) Then fold the sleeve across the core, wrapping any extra material around the curve of the core. Repeat for the other sleeve. (Illustration I.) Continue down through the layers, wrapping each around the core and smoothing out wrinkles. (Illustration J.) Pack as tightly as you can. Make sure you fold the bottom of the garment up first and then each sleeve; do not interweave garments with one another.

After the last layer is folded over, secure the straps to keep your wardrobe in place. Do not cinch them too tightly.

Shoes — You have space for one pair of shoes in this section and one in the other section. Place shoe bags along the bottom of the case next to the bundle. If they are flat, place the heels in the corners of the bag with soles facing the hinge. (Illustration K.) Place high heels diagonally inward. The heel should not face the hinge or the clothing. If you have large shoes, try placing them with the toes at an angle, cut

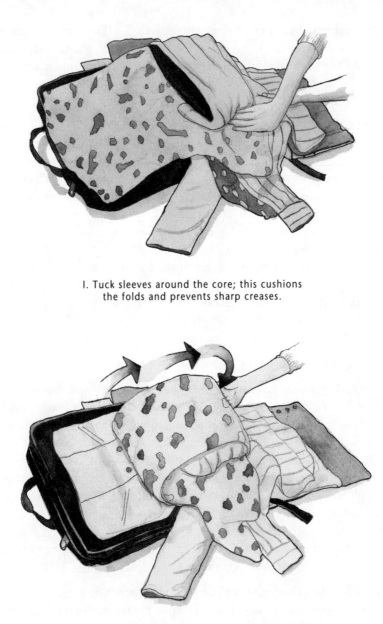

I. Tuck sleeves around the core; this cushions the folds and prevents sharp creases.

J. Fold hems around the core; continue with each layer.

K. The finished bundle. Place shoes along bottom
edge of bag; tuck belt around the zippered rim.

down on the number of pairs you take, or use accessory space or that second totebag.

Belts — Place belts along the inside zippered rim of the suitcase. (Illustration K.)

Ties — Can be handled in a number of ways. If you want nice, crisp ties, buy a tie case that fits the measurements of the bag, and lay it on top of the bundle. You can also use a stiff piece of cardboard and wrap the ties around it, securing them with a rubber band. Or, for those ties you *might* use if you get into that four-star restaurant in Paris, simply wrap them around the finished bundle.

Accessible items — Now take those items you kept out of the bundle for easy access. Lay these on top of the bundle or tucked in the corners outside of the bundle. Such items might include the next day's socks and underwear, a folded nightgown, a swimsuit, shorts and a T-shirt, or a sweater.

SHORTCUTS

Sometimes lack of time, impatience, or concern about wrinkling creates the desire for a slightly faster method of packing. Here are two methods that I like. Experiment with them and see if you like them better.

Quick Fix Bundle Method — Perfect for the way home. Lay all the items in the suitcase, with collars and waistbands stacked in the same direction. Drape all sides as you would if you were using the perfectionist's method. Place the core in the middle. Now take all the bottoms at once and fold them over the core, wrapping them around if need be. Do the same with the left sleeves. Voila! There is your bundle. The difference is that the outer edges are not as nicely built and the sides of the garments will wrinkle. But, if you are in a hurry or on your way home, who cares?

Packing on hangers: The Z-fold Method — This option is for packing suits, dresses, and other outfits in a carry-on suitcase (with or without suiter option), garment bag, or even a duffel bag. The outfits are hung on wire hangers, encased in plastic dry-cleaning bags, and packed into the bag. The plastic reduces wrinkling by eliminating friction, making this the preferred packing method when wrinkle-free clothing is a top priority. It is also convenient to arrive in the hotel and hang the clothes right up. The downside is that you cannot fit in as many items of clothing when you pack this way. The clothing cannot be packed too tightly without defeating the purpose.

Hang your outfit on one hanger: pants or skirt over bar, then shirt/blouse, then jacket. Pull the shirt sleeves through the jacket sleeves. Stuff with tissue paper if you like. Cross the jacket sleeves in front. Cover with a plastic dry-cleaning bag, and tuck in the hanger. Lay the shoulders of the jacket against the hinge end of the bag. Pick up both sides of the midsection of the jacket and bring the midsection up to the shoulders in a "Z"-fold. Tuck any hem underneath. Voila! The suit fits into your bag, and you're packed.

For bags with the suiter option, hook the hanger on the clip, lay out the jacket, then do a "Z"-fold.

For a duffel bag, it's a bit different—put the outfits on hangers, roll each in thirds horizontally, and lay into the duffel.

Unpacking

When you arrive at your hotel, unfurl the bundle and let the garments drape over the sides of the bag. This will give them a chance to breathe and rest. Hang them up if you will be staying a few days. You will find it is easy to insert the hangers while the clothes are still in the bag. To repack, you will not have to fold much, just lay the garments in quickly. Nor will you have to iron, so you will save even more time in the long run.

GETTING CLOTHES IN AND OUT

If you have packed only separates, it is easy to unfurl two or three garments, reach inside the bundle to grab the one you need, slip it out, and repack. If you have packed longer items such as a dress, you will have more to unwrap. This is another reason for packing separates only!

▼ Packing Your Travel Gear

Now the clothing is taken care of. What about toiletries, personal items, appliances, more shoes, small purse, raincoat, umbrella, etc.? Where you put these items will differ according to the suitcase you have. The following instructions are for packing specific types of suitcases. Find the one that applies to your luggage.

- ▼ Make sure to pack toiletries in tight, high-quality bottles. Fill three quarters full, squeeze out air, and close. Wrap in plastic bags and store in organizer pouches away from clothing.

- ▼ Consider the placement of your gear according to the access you'll need during different phases of your trip. You'll probably be transferring things around as you go. Below are some suggestions for placement.

  For more tips on accessories, see chapter 3.

▼ Packing a Three-Compartment Carry-on with Two Wardrobes

The instructions that follow are for packing a 21- or 22-inch–long bag that has three full-length compartments, such as the Easy Going Special Edition Bag. This configuration is the most convenient for multipurpose and multiclimate trips because it allows you to organize your clothing according to purpose and season. The deepest section will hold your wardrobe bundle for business and cold weather, the second will hold a minimalist leisure and warm-weather wardrobe, the third will contain all your other accessories. Note: You need a core pouch for each separate bundle.

Section 1

Make a bundle with your dress or cold-weather clothes. Put the bundle in the deepest section of the bag.

Section 2

This compartment will hold casual or warm-weather items, if applicable. When you have a second wardrobe, make a separate bundle, arranging your casual jacket, skirts, slacks, long-sleeved shirts, T-shirts, and walking shorts in that order. Assemble the related underwear, socks, and other wardrobe accessories in the core pouch.

Section 3

This compartment will hold all of your other accessories—everything that is not part of your wardrobe. Use this compartment for your packable raincoat and umbrella, toiletry kit or dopp kit, laundry kit, medical kit, collapsible bag, Packtowl, hairdryer, iron or steamer, water purification items, flask, packable purse or fanny pack (stuffed with odds and ends such as immersion heater, money exchange calculator, and so on), books and maps, converter and adapters. Think of this space as four or five vertical columns, running from the bottom hinge to the top. This is an efficient use of the space.

Pack the columns in stacks from front to back, with flat items toward the middle and irregular shapes toward the outside. Pack all the heavy items at the bottom of the bag, with light objects on top. Because your toiletry or shave kit is fourteen or fifteen inches high, it will stand in the suitcase vertically. Your packable raincoat and umbrella go here. Cushion objects such as hairdryers with the raincoat.

▼ Packing a Three-Compartment Carry-on with One Wardrobe

If you have only one basic wardrobe, you will probably be able to fit all the garments in the middle section of the bag. This gives you lots of flexibility for using the other two side pockets. Put your accessories in one side compartment . In the other, you can put your dirty laundry, clothing (such as a sweater), items you want quick access to, extra shoes, or business papers.

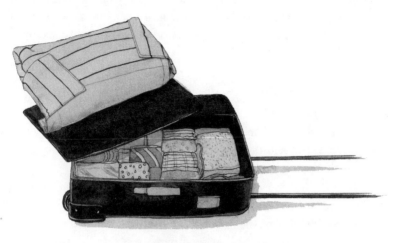

One-compartment bag, with accessories
in bottom, then partition, then bundle.
Accessibles are laid on top.

▼ Packing a One-Compartment Suitcase (21–24 inches) with or without "Suiter" Option

Standard pullman cases and wheelaboards have only one deep section. Some include a partition, making it a two-compartment bag. Popular "suiter" bags have a section in which you can hang a suit or jacket.

The best way to pack such bags is in three layers: a bottom layer made up of your accessories, irregularly shaped objects, and shoes; a middle layer made up of the bundle; and a top layer of "accessibles"—anything you want quick access to on arrival.

1. Open your suitcase. On the floor of the bag, place your personal items, appliances, laundry kit, first-aid kit, shoes, small purse (stuffed with kits or other items), water purifier kit, etc. Heaviest items should go toward the edge that will touch the ground when the bag is put down.

   You can also roll up extra socks, T-shirts, leggings, and other soft garments to fill gaps and prevent items from rolling.

Hint: To keep the accessories from moving about and create a smooth surface for packing the bundle, buy a package of light- to medium-weight, nonwoven interfacing (the brand name is Pellon) at a fabric store. Each piece is 3 yards long by 22 inches wide. Cut a piece double the length of your suitcase and fold it in half. Lay it over the accessories, in effect creating a sectional divider. Tuck the edges down around the sides of the bag, enclosing the accessories and creating a shelf.

2. Make your bundle as described on pp. 105–113.

3. Lay your "accessibles" on top of the bundle. I put in a big T-shirt, nightgown, or sweater face up, fold both arms across horizontally, and fold the garment in half, bringing the bottom up to the shoulders. I lay a pair of walking shorts vertically.

4. For "suiters," layer slacks or skirt over the hanger bar, then hang a shirt and layer the jacket over it, pulling the sleeves through. Cover it with a plastic dry cleaning bag. Use supplied cushioning bars to cushion folds, or use your own socks or rolled tissue paper to do so. Cross sleeves inward in front of the jacket and fasten supplied straps across the jacket.

5. Outside pockets. Depending on configuration, pack these with quick access items and liquids like medicine, makeup, toiletries, packable raincoat and umbrella, hat, water bottle, and items such as inflatable pillows, eyeshades, and earplugs to be used on the plane. Or, pack with computer, business materials, etc.

How to Pack Folded Shirts — Businesspeople often prefer to travel with folded shirts. You can pack shirts folded from the laundry, or you can fold your own. To fold your own shirts and pack them wrinkle free, check out a great product called the SHIRT-Frame by the Stuffed SHIRT company. This unique packing aid employs the same principle as the Bundle Method of packing—that clothes wrapped around a soft edge and kept under tension will not crease or wrinkle. The Shirt-Frame consists of an 8 × 10-inch polypropelene frame with a "rolling hinge"—a curved bottom edge around which you fold your shirt (complete, easy to use instructions are provided). It also comes with an adjustable collar ring, which keeps the collar stiff and neat. Also available is a TIE-Frame, a similar piece around which you wrap your ties.

Best for casual shirts, Eagle Creek also makes "Pack-it," a packing aid which holds folded and stacked shirts.

If you travel regularly with folded shirts, look for luggage that has a separate compartment for shirts. For example, Atlantic offers a suiter with a mesh compartment in the lid for shirts.

Here is a method for packing folded shirts when using the Bundle Method of packing:

1. Follow the above instructions through number 1.

2. Make a small bundle of slacks, knit shirts, etc.

3. Place folded shirts on top.

4. For suiters follow directions as above for hanging jacket or suit.

OR:

1. Put travel gear in a separate, smaller bag.

2. Make a bundle on the bottom level of the bag.

3. Put your shirts on top of the bundle.

▼ Packing a Two-Compartment Carry-on

For the two-compartment suitcase, you do not need to make a divider. Typically the bag has a partition for organizing contents into separate compartments and is most suitable for a single-bundle wardrobe.

1. Pack section one, the bottom side, with accessories, irregular objects, and shoes as you would the one-compartment bag.

2. Pack section two, the top side, with the bundle and shoes.

3. Lay whatever you want access to on top of the bundle. Tuck socks and underwear in the corners of the bag.

▼ Packing a Travel Pack (Convertible Backpack)

Travel packs require a different technique because you have to take weight distribution into consideration. For general travel, heavy items should be carried on top and closer to your back. Lighter items such as clothing should be packed toward the bottom and away from your back. However, if you are doing hiking and climbing, a lower center of gravity is needed. Pack heavy items in the middle, close to your back. Use the inside cinch straps to help keep the pack balanced and items in place. The bag will usually contains clothing, some travel accessories, and shoes. There are two ways to pack a convertible pack—the Bundle Method and the roll-and-stuff method.

Bundle Method —

1. Make a bundle of your clothes, keeping aside what you want quick access to (a sweater, and so on). Lay the bundle in the well of the bag toward the bottom near the waistband. Secure it with tie straps.

2. Nest one shoe inside the other and place the pair along the top edge of the bag (if you are carrying your bag vertically, this will be near your head).

3. Place accessories and kits at the north end of the bundle and around the top edges, using organizers such as color-coded stuff sacks or nylon pouches. Heavier items should be clustered toward the top edge, close to your back.

4. Place items you need to reach quickly, such as a rainjacket, on top of the accessories near the zippers. Also pack accessibles in outside pockets.

Roll-and-Stuff Method —

1. Roll your clothes and place them in color-coded stuff sacks, one each for clean clothes, dirty clothes, city clothes, hiking clothes, and so on. Accessories can go in pouches, stuff sacks, or Ziploc bags.

2. Place lighter items, such as clothing sacks, at the south end of the bag. Place a jacket or sweater at the north end.

3. Place equipment and shoes at the north end on top of the jacket, away from the back. (If you are climbing and hiking, this is

reversed—lighter items go higher and farther from your back, and heavier items go in the middle, closer to your back.)

4. Place items you need to retrieve quickly should be placed around the edge, in outside pockets, and near the zippers. Always put things back in the same place, so you can find them in the dark and avoid forgetting things. Note: A rain cover is a good item to have if you expect to walk in the rain. (For a great book on back-packing, read *Hiking and Backpacking: A Complete Guide,* by Karen Berger (W. W. Norton, 1995).

▼ Packing a Garment Bag

Optional handy supplies to keep things in tip-top shape:

- ▼ Cardboard hanger extenders—available at good dry cleaning stores. (These give added support to suit shoulders on wire hangers.)

- ▼ Plastic dry cleaning bags—hang over suits, jackets, dresses. These reduce friction and let clothing drape naturally.

Tissue paper helps ease creases caused by folds. You can stuff layers of tissue paper under draped slacks and stuff collars and sleeves.

1. If you have one, put the cardboard extension on the hanger. Hang pants over the bar, and a skirt on top of the slacks.

2. Hang a sweater or shirt on the hanger. Then hang the jacket on top. Pull the shirtsleeves through. Smooth collars. Cross the sleeves in front of the jacket.

3. Cover with a dry cleaning bag and hang in the garment bag.

4. Pack the hangers holding easily wrinkled items such as blouses and shirts toward the back of the bag to cushion the horizontal crease when the bag is folded in half.

5. Try to store the bag hanging or lying flat.

▼ Packing Larger (Checkable) Suitcases

Sometimes you have too many things to bring to limit yourself to a carry-on–size bag, or you can't be bothered with carry-on. Go to town!

The best way to pack pullmans is in three layers: a bottom layer made up of your accessories, irregularly shaped objects, rolled items, and shoes; a middle layer made up of clothing; and a top layer of "accessibles"—anything you want quick access to on arrival.

1. Open your suitcase. On the floor of the bag place your appliances, books, laundry kit, first aid kit, shoes, gifts, small purse (stuffed with kits or other items), water purifier kit, etc. Heaviest items should go toward the edge that will touch the ground when the bag is put down. Fill spaces with rolled-up knits, T-shirts, leggings, hosiery, and other casual garments to fill gaps and prevent items from moving.

2. Layer 2 — Wardrobe items:

   Method 1: Hang jackets, dresses, suits, and shirts together on hangers. Encase in plastic dry cleaning bags. Use the "Z"-fold (see p. 114) or lay them flat for a 26-inch suitcase.

   Method 2: Interfolding method (If desired, cover each item with dry cleaning bags):

   Using alternate directions (left and right), lay the upper half of long items such as slacks, dresses, and full skirts (folded vertically on each side) in the case horizontally. Drape bottom halves over the opposite side of the case. (If the case is very large, items may lie flat.)

   Lay the upper half of sweaters, blouses, straight skirts, and jackets vertically in the case, draping the bottom of the garments over the edge. (This is the perfect place to stash breakable or fragile items!)

   Now flip the draped portions of the clothing into the case.

   Tuck socks, underwear, and other soft items around the edge where needed to fill spaces.

   Pack your coat on top, using the interfolding method above.

3. Lay your "accessibles" on top of the bundle. I put in a big T-shirt, nightgown, or sweater face up, fold both arms across horizontally, and fold the garment in half, bringing the bottom up to the shoulders. You might put a pair of shorts here, too.

▼ Packing a Duffel Bag

By popular demand, here's how to pack a duffel bag. You can get a lot in a small space. Always pack a duffel snugly. Fill the corners. Duffels are best suited for casual clothing, although it is possible to roll up garments on a hanger encased in dry cleaning bags and place them into a large duffel on top of heavy items.

Place heavy items (books, appliances, gear, shoes, etc.) along the bottom of the bag. Stuff shoes with socks, etc., and place in shoe bags. Roll T-shirts, knits, jeans, etc., and make a layer of these. On top, place shirts, blouses, and sweaters folded once across the middle, sleeves folded inward. Or, you can put these items on hangers in a plastic dry cleaning bag and fold in thirds or a "Z" fold (p. 114). (These two layers can be interchanged depending on which items you want better access to.) On top place raincoat or jacket.

▼ Packing a Totebag or Daypack

Keep in mind the sequence of your needs when packing your second bag. This bag can bear more weight since you will most likely put it under your seat and not overhead. To avoid losing items, try to return them to their proper place.

Outside pockets —

- ▼ Boarding passes, customs documents, local currency, and any other items you need accessible for boarding and leaving the plane or train. (Don't forget that your passport, ID, etc. is in your security wallet!)
- ▼ Pen and notebook
- ▼ Emergency items: knife, flashlight, umbrella, hat, tools, compass

- ▼ In-flight toiletry kit: moist towelettes, toilet-seat covers, tampons, mints, toothbrush and toothpaste, floss, comb, lip balm, moisturizer, headache reliever, Band-Aids
- ▼ Snack/water bottle

On top near the zipper –
- ▼ Medicine, cup, water bottle; eyeglasses, sunglasses
- ▼ In-flight materials: laptop (fully charged), business papers, reading materials, walkman with tapes, maps, guidebook, and so on.
- ▼ In-flight travel accessories
- ▼ Thick socks for the plane

Bottom —

At the bottom, place valuables, clothing, and other necessities you will not need frequently.

- ▼ Sweater or jacket, umbrella, keys, camera and film, half of your traveler's checks, a change of clothing, gifts, breakables

6

Business Travel

For businesspeople, carry-on luggage has many benefits. It gives you more control over your trip and schedule by eliminating the possibility of lost luggage and allowing you to avoid the carousel and get right to your hotel or meeting. Traveling light and remaining mobile with your hands free also enables you to make phone calls, open doors, and write easily. Mobility also reduces the risk of becoming a target for pickpockets and thieves while standing around waiting for luggage.

Perfect appearance is often the highest priority for business travelers. For that reason, I recommend the careful selection of fabrics, choosing the right luggage, and the use of plastic dry cleaning bags in some instances to help battle wrinkles on the road. Of course, if your hotels offer 24-hour clothing care services, and amenities such as irons, adapter plugs, hairdryers, and toiletries, you can pack less and still feel confident that you'll be able to maintain your appearance on the road.

In this section, I offer business wardrobes for different types of trips. Use the following guidelines to make leaving on a business trip routine.

▼ Set Yourself Up for Success

- ▼ Choose the right luggage. With the right bags on hand, you will be prepared for any type of trip. I recommend:
- ▼ A 22-inch wheelaboard "suiter" (with or without "portable office" features) or a 3-compartment suitcase. Either of these will suffice for short trips with 1 or 2 jackets and coordinated separates (use a luggage cart if necessary). Also great for vacation travel.
- ▼ A hanging garment bag (2–4 suit capacity for longer trips and lots of clothes, or a simple, lightweight garment cover for that one tuxedo, suit, or evening dress).

▼ A smaller briefcase, shoulder bag, or small duffel for your glasses, toiletries, makeup, medicine, cell phone, computer and equipment, CD player and headphones, work and reading materials, itinerary and travel documents, office supplies, water bottle, and spare shirt and underwear, in case your main bag is separated from you.

See chapter 2 for further descriptions of these bags.

▼ Traveling with a Laptop Computer

Even though laptops are extremely portable, traveling with a laptop isn't as easy as it looks, especially for the international traveler. It pays to know all the issues before you decide to bring yours.

First, the weight issue. Invest in the lightest weight laptop that you can, because you may be carrying a battery pack, a back-up battery pack, a charger, cabling, disks and CD's, and other various equipment.

Second, be aware of your power needs, what it takes to plug in. Most computers run in the United States on 110 volts, but you will need a converter if the foreign voltage is 220 volts. Some computers are dual-voltage models. You may need to add a heavy-duty transformer for prolonged use. You will also need the proper adapter plugs for the wall sockets. You can buy adapter plugs with or without grounding plugs.

Hooking the modem up to the phone line is the next project. Since many foreign countries don't use an RJ-11 jack, you may need a phone jack adapter so that your modem can be plugged in to the local phone jack. (You may need a different one for each country you travel to!) Or, your hotel might not even have a phone jack, but may be hard-wired. You might have to connect through the handset.

In fact, there can be several connectivity obstacles: hard-wired phones, different dial tones, pulse dialing, digital phone systems, PBX systems, bad lines and other modem-defying technology. Not to mention finding an ISP or dealing with high phone charges.

Suffice it to say that you need to be prepared. Fortunately for the mobile traveler there is a website that can answer all your questions and help you get connected abroad. It also sells all the equipment you might need for the countries you are visiting. Lookup www.teleadapt.com (see Resources). Another source is www.warrior.com.

Take lots of batteries or the extra battery pack if you have a flight longer than 2 hours. Future trend: some (usually long-haul) airlines are now equipping themselves with "laptop friendly" seats. You need an in-flight adapter which will allow you to plug your computer into a 12 volt DC power supply built into certain airline seats. To find out more about this, contact Teleadapt and register with their Airpower Database. They will keep you posted on the adapter, and also all airlines and seats that offer airpower.

▼ The Business Travel Wardrobe

Traveling for business requires careful focus. Your wardrobe must present you in the best possible image in all your activities, yet still be travelworthy. If you will be moving around a great deal and meeting with different people, you can take the minimalist wardrobe, laundering as you go. If you will be seeing the same people constantly, you will require the moderate or luxury wardrobes. You may find a hanging suit bag necessary.

Here are a few guidelines to make business packing a breeze:

▼ Make a packing list. Take into account destination dress codes, climate, and activities (see pp. 92–93). Write down two to three completely accessorized outfits. They should all coordinate with each other. Use your list for each trip, then refine it for the next one.

▼ Keep your packing list(s) stored on your computer and leave a hard copy in your suitcase for the next trip.

▼ Choose fabrics carefully. Invest in packable light- or medium-weight wool suits, merino wool or silk knits, cottons, cotton/polyester dress shirts and casual slacks, washed silk, and linen (see chapter 4 for more details).

▼ Stick to one or two coordinating neutrals. Make one a dark neutral that will be suitable for day or evening—black, navy, gray, or brown. The second should be a lighter coordinating color such as white, gray, ivory, or khaki. Use accent colors, such as burgundy, red, and other brights, for shirts and blouses. Shoes, belts, and handbags should be in your basic neutral colors.

▼ Try to pack items that can double for daywear and casualwear.

▼ Pack a dress shirt for each business day, up to five shirts. Choose high quality cotton and polyester pinpoints and oxfords (available from Land's End) if possible. Pack shirts hanging or folded, as you prefer (see chapter 5). All dress shirts are uncooperative to pack!

▼ Pack a pair of hose for each business day, plus a spare pair. Launder hose before wearing them to decrease likelihood of runs.

▼ Purchase thermal silk underwear in styles suitable for business attire if traveling in cold weather.

▼ Pack using plastic dry cleaning bags, cardboard hanger supports, and tissue paper, available at dry cleaning stores. (See chapter 5.)

▼ Always find out if your hotel offers 24-hour laundry service, and amenities such as irons, adapter plugs, hairdryers, and toiletries. If they do, pack less!

▼ Pack slip-on garment shields to cut down on laundry.

▼ Always take a swimsuit or activewear for the hotel gym.

▼ Store your valuables and money in a security wallet (see chapter 4).

▼ Women's Business Travel Wardrobes

Business Suit Wardrobe for Women

This wardrobe is for the woman who wears suits during the day and has special dinners or other events in the evening. All items should coordinate.

MINIMALIST

Layer 1 – Underlayer

▼ 3-6 pairs of underpants (3 if you will wash, 6 if not)

▼ 2 bras

- ▼ 1-2 sets of garment shields
- ▼ Silk knit undershirt or camisole to wear under blouses if cold
- ▼ Above-the-knee silk shorts to wear under skirts if cold
- ▼ 1 half-slip (optional)
- ▼ 1 extra-large T-shirt or cover-up for sleepwear and pool *or* pajamas *or* nightgown
- ▼ Bathing suit with cover-up (optional)

Layer 2 – Clothing

- ▼ 1 suit
- ▼ 2 blouses (both day-into-evening)
- ▼ 1 two-piece dress that coordinates with the suit or 1 simple shirt-waist dress in a coordinating neutral tone

Layer 3 – Outerlayer

- ▼ 1 raincoat and umbrella, if needed

Layer 4 – Extremities

- ▼ 1 pair of walking pumps
- ▼ 1 pair of dress pumps for evening
- ▼ 3 pairs of hose for day (or one for each business day)
- ▼ 2 pairs of hose for evening (sheer)
- ▼ Thongs for pool, if needed
- ▼ Athletic shoes or sneakers, if needed
- ▼ Athletic clothing and underwear, if needed

Accessories

- ▼ 2 scarves
- ▼ Jewelry (earrings, brooch, necklaces)
- ▼ 1 evening handbag

MODERATE

To the minimalist wardrobe add:

- ▼ 1 suit
- ▼ 1 blouse

LUXURY

To the moderate wardrobe add:

▼ 1 two-piece dress *or* other dress, for evening wear

▼ 1 pair of evening shoes

▼ Accessories for evening wear

Business Coordinates Wardrobe for Women

Classic-looking coordinates are for women who do not need business suits but must look professional. All items should be day-into-evening styles. Pack the Business Suit Wardrobe (above), with the following substitutions:

MINIMALIST

Layer 2 – Clothing

▼ 1 simple jacket (unstructured type)

▼ 1 skirt, tailored style (*or* 1 pair of slacks)

▼ 1 two-piece dress *or* 1 chemise-type or shirtwaist dress

▼ 1 or 2 blouses (one for day or evening)

Layer 4 – Extremities

▼ 3 scarves (1 shawl, 1 long rectangular, 1 square) (optional)

▼ Simple jewelry (gold, pearls, necklaces)

▼ 1 or 2 leather belts

▼ Day handbag (or use briefcase)

▼ Small shoulder bag for day or evening

▼ 3 pairs of hose for day (more if you don't want to wash)

▼ 2 pairs of hose for evening (sheer)

▼ 1 pair of walking pumps in a neutral color

▼ 1 pair of pumps for evening, if needed

▼ Thongs for pool, if needed

MODERATE

To the minimalist wardrobe add:

▼ 1 skirt *or* 1 pair of slacks

▼ 1 cardigan sweater (V-neck, to wear alone and with others)

LUXURY

For special events, add to the moderate wardrobe:

▼ 1 more jacket *or* 1 dress

▼ 1 pair of shoes for a special outfit

▼ Accessories for a special outfit

Combined Business and Leisure Wardrobe for Women

Clothes for casual activities after your business trip are easily included in your carry-on bag. If you are on the move and need room in your suitcase, send your suits home by Federal Express or UPS after the meetings are over.

To the minimalist business wardrobes listed above, add the following for casual wear:

▼ 1 pair of casual slacks

▼ 1 pair of knee-length shorts (optional)

▼ 1 skirt (optional)

▼ 2 casual shirts, such as a matching blouse and tank top

▼ 1 pair of athletic or walking shoes

▼ 2 or 3 pairs of casual socks

▼ Activewear for golf, tennis, and so on, as needed

Off-site Business and Casual Wardrobe for Women

Sometimes, at a week-long conference held at a resort, there will be business seminars or meetings during the day, dressier events at night, and a company barbecue on the weekend. This is the hardest trip to plan for because you need clothes for a variety of situations. You will be seeing the same people every day, so you will probably want to take a few more clothes. Casual in such settings does not mean T-shirt and jeans; wardrobe protocol must still be observed. Your best-looking casual clothing should be carefully chosen. If you wear the suit or casual outfit on the plane, you should be able to pack this entire wardrobe (which is in a black, khaki, and burgundy color scheme) in one carry-on suitcase and a shoulder bag. Or, if you prefer, use a garment bag. For this wardrobe, pack the Business Suit Wardrobe (pp. 128–130), with the following substitutions:

Layer 2 – Clothing

▼ 1 jacket and skirt *or* a suit, black (for day meetings and evening)

▼ 1 skirt, khaki

▼ 1 pair of black silk slacks, for evening

▼ 1 plain cream-colored blouse (day or evening)

▼ 1 burgundy blouse (day or evening)

▼ 1 two-piece dress in a print, black and khaki (or black, khaki, and burgundy if you can find it) *or* one shirtwaist dress (day or evening)

▼ 1 burgundy cardigan or sweater set

▼ 1 pair of khaki slacks (for the barbecue)

▼ 1 casual top (for the barbecue; can be one half of the sweater set)

Layer 3 – Outerlayer

▼ 1 windbreaker, if needed

Layer 4 – Extremities

▼ 2 pairs of casual socks

▼ 1 burgundy belt

▼ 1 pair of black pumps (business)

▼ 1 pair of burgundy loafers *or* oxford-type shoes (for the barbecue)

▼ Thongs *or* light sandals for the pool, if needed

Accessories

▼ 3 scarves (1 shawl, 1 long rectangle, 1 square) (optional)

▼ Simple jewelry (gold, pearls, necklaces)

- ▼ Day handbag
- ▼ Small shoulder bag for evening
- ▼ 3 pairs of hose for day (more if you don't want to wash)
- ▼ 2 pairs of hose for evening (sheer)

▼ Men's Business Travel Wardrobes

Regular Business Wardrobe for Men

If you will be meeting with different people every day, you can keep your clothing to a minimum. If you are with the same people constantly, you will need a few more shirts and a second suit.

MINIMALIST

Layer 1 – Underlayer

- ▼ 3-8 pairs of undershorts
- ▼ Silk knit thermal undershirt and bottoms to wear if cold
- ▼ 1 extra-large T-shirt for cover-up and sleepwear, *or* 1 pair of pajamas
- ▼ Swim trunks, if needed

Layer 2 – Clothing

- ▼ 1 suit
- ▼ 1 pair of matching slacks (to double as casual wear)
- ▼ 3-5 dress shirts (3 if you send laundry out, or take 1 shirt for each business day)
- ▼ 1 or 2 casual shirts, such as polo-type

Layer 3 – Outerlayer

- ▼ 1 raincoat and umbrella, if needed

Layer 4 – Extremities

- ▼ 3-5 pairs of dress socks (1 for each day of the trip)
- ▼ 2 ties *or* 1 tie for each day of the trip
- ▼ 1 belt

- ▼ 1 pair of dress shoes
- ▼ 1 pair of athletic shoes, if needed
- ▼ Athletic clothing (T-shirt, shorts, underwear, socks, nylon warmup suit), if needed

MODERATE

For trips of one week or more, to the minimalist wardrobe add:

- ▼ 1 suit or a blazer

LUXURY

If you are planning to take a garment bag, to the moderate wardrobe add:

- ▼ 1 suit *or* tuxedo

Combined Business and Casual Wardrobe for Men

Try using patterned socks, motif ties, a patterned sweater, or sports shirts to bring variety into the wardrobe, which is based on a color scheme.

Layer 1 – Underlayer

- ▼ 3-8 pairs of undershorts
- ▼ Silk knit thermal undershirt and bottoms to wear if cold
- ▼ 1 extra-large T-shirt for cover-up and sleepwear, *or* 1 pair of pajamas
- ▼ Swim trunks, if needed

Layer 2 – Clothing

- ▼ 1 dark suit (optional in some settings)
- ▼ 1 navy blazer
- ▼ 1 dress shirt for each business day (at least one white) with ties
- ▼ 2 pairs of slacks, 1 gray, 1 khaki (the latter doubles as casual)

- ▼ 1 pullover or cardigan sweater (cordovan V- or crew-neck, print or pattern)
- ▼ 2 casual shirts (striped, patterned, or polo-type)

Layer 3 – Outerlayer

- ▼ 1 raincoat and umbrella, if needed

Layer 4 – Extremities

- ▼ 5 pairs of dress socks (1 for each day of the trip if not washing)
- ▼ 1 belt, black
- ▼ 1 pair of dress shoes, black
- ▼ 1 pair of casual loafers or oxfords, cordovan
- ▼ Thongs for pool, if needed
- ▼ Athletic clothing (underwear, socks, and shoes), if needed
- ▼ Cufflinks, tie clips, other accessories as needed

▼ Security

Travelers on business trips can be targets for theft and terrorist crimes. If you are traveling internationally, it pays to avoid being identified as a business traveler. Carry inconspicuous softsided luggage. Briefcases and computers should be kept with you at all times and packed inconspicuously. Pack your backup disks separately from the computer for extra security. For more about the subject, see chapter 10.

▼ Checklist for Business Travel

- ☐ security wallet and contents (see pp. 36–39)
- ☐ laptop bag/briefcase/sample case/luggage cart
- ☐ business cards
- ☐ calculator
- ☐ cellphone/charger

- [ ] computer equipment (see p. 59)
- [ ] expense ledger
- [ ] pager
- [ ] personal organizer; appointments, schedule, addresses and phone numbers, calendar
- [ ] business papers/files
- [ ] itinerary
- [ ] frequent flyer/rental car/discount/gym membership vouchers and cards
- [ ] confirmations and vouchers
- [ ] convention pre-registration and name tags
- [ ] notepad/pen/business stationery/envelopes
- [ ] other office supplies (see pp. 58–59)
- [ ] travel steamer or iron (dual-voltage with adapters for foriegn travel)
- [ ] mints
- [ ] other _____

7

Active Travel and Adventure Wardrobes

Okay—you've read all the basics. Now let's put some wardrobes together for your next trip. In this chapter are simple packing lists for leisure and adventure vacations. Use them as guidelines to help you prepare for your trip. The sample packing lists are organized by layer because I believe that every traveler should get in the habit of thinking—"Do I have what I need for Layer 1? Layer 2?" etc. (See chapter 4 for details on layering.) Provided are moderate, minimalist, and luxury packing lists.

Let's start with the Basic Moderate Carry-on Wardrobe. For the "moderate" packer, which includes most of us, eight to ten basic garments will create more than twenty different looks. It is basically one week's worth of clothing. If you figure that you will wash once a week with a handwash in between, this wardrobe is good for any length trip, from one week to one year! You determine what the style will be—very casual, semi-casual, or dressy. Vary bottom pieces according to your preference. All pieces should coordinate.

For more on building a travel wardrobe, see chapter 4.

▼ The Basic Moderate Carry-on Wardrobe for Women

The basic nine or ten garments:

▼ 1 jacket (blazer or casual)

▼ 1 skirt that coordinates with the jacket

- ▼ 1 pair slacks that matches or coordinates with the jacket
- ▼ 1 extra bottom piece—skirt or pants (casual)
- ▼ 1 long-sleeved shirt
- ▼ 2 additional shirts or blouses
- ▼ 1 outfit suitable for both casual and dressy occasions: a two-piece dress (a blouse and skirt made of the same fabric, which can be a print) with a matching belt or sash, *or* a skirt or slacks and blouse, *or* a simple dress
- ▼ 1 cardigan sweater

Believe it or not, this moderate wardrobe can be worn in at least fifteen different ways.

A SAMPLE PACKING LIST—WOMEN'S MODERATE WARDROBE

Your packing list for a moderate wardrobe, organized by layer, would look like this:

Layer 1 – Underlayer

- ▼ 1 or 2 T-shirts (in cold weather substitute a long-sleeved turtle-neck)
- ▼ 1 extra-large T-shirt for sleepwear or to use as a cover-up in warm weather *or* 1 set of thermal silk or polyester-knit long underwear (for cold weather)
- ▼ 2-8 sets of underwear (4-5 is average)
- ▼ 1 or 2 sets of garment shields
- ▼ 1 half-slip, if needed
- ▼ 2 bras
- ▼ 1 swimsuit

Layer 2 – Clothing

- ▼ 1 coordinating jacket, skirt, and pair of slacks
- ▼ 1 pair casual slacks or skirt

- ▼ 1 two-piece dress *or* 1 simple dress *or* 1 blouse and a pair of slacks *or* 1 skirt and a blouse
- ▼ 1 or 2 blouses, shirts, or blouse-type sweaters; at least 1 long-sleeved
- ▼ 1 cardigan sweater
- ▼ 1 pair walking shorts (optional)
- ▼ Athletic clothing and underwear, if needed

Layer 3 – Outerlayer/Raingear

- ▼ 1 raincoat *or* windbreaker

Layer 4 – Extremities

- ▼ 4–5 pairs of hose
- ▼ 4–5 pairs of thin to medium-weight socks (fast dry/solid moisture wicking)
- ▼ 2 pairs of sock liners
- ▼ 1 pair of dress shoes (low pumps or dressy flats)
- ▼ 1 pair of sandals or thongs
- ▼ 1 pair of walking or athletic shoes
- ▼ Sun hat, rain hat
- ▼ Gloves, if needed

Accessories

- ▼ 1 or 2 belts
- ▼ 2 or 3 scarves (1 large square shawl, 1 large square, 1 long rectangular)
- ▼ Simple jewelry (a few basic pieces, but nothing valuable)
- ▼ 1 umbrella

The Minimalist Wardrobe for Women

The minimalist wardrobe is ideal for short or warm-weather trips. It can be adapted for business or casual wear. If you like, add a pair of walking shorts.

The basic six or seven garments, which can be mixed and matched however you like:

- ▼ 1 jacket *or* a cardigan
- ▼ 1 matching skirt that coordinates with the jacket
- ▼ 1 pair of slacks that matches or coordinates with the jacket
- ▼ 1 long-sleeved shirt
- ▼ 1 more bottom piece
- ▼ 1 outfit suitable for both casual and dressy occasions: a two-piece dress (a blouse and skirt made of the same fabric, which can be a print) with a matching belt or sash, *or* a simple dress, *or* a skirt or a pair of slacks and a blouse

To make a packing list for the minimalist wardrobe, use the one provided on pp. 138–139 for the moderate wardrobe, substituting these basic garments for Layer 2.

The Luxury Wardrobe for Women

The luxury wardrobe will give you the most variety (and the heaviest bag!). It is an expansion of the moderate wardrobe with the addition of two or three items for evening wear, repeated business affairs, or special events. If the fabrics and colors of the extra garments coordinate with all the others and are suitable for day or evening wear (silk, wool crepe, rayon blends), your wardrobe will expand exponentially.

The additional items are:

- ▼ 1 additional jacket *or*
- ▼ 1 suit with a blouse (that coordinates with your other clothing), *or*
- ▼ 1 two-piece dress with a jacket, *or*
- ▼ 1 blouse, 1 pair of slacks, and a cardigan, *or*
- ▼ 1 special-event outfit

For the suit, select a solid color or a tweed that coordinates with the original three-piece outfit. Choose an extra blouse in a different style. Keep in mind that you are taking only one additional outfit, not all four—you still plan to carry-on your bag!

To make up a packing list, use the one provided for the moderate wardrobe.

▼ The Basic Moderate Carry-on Wardrobe for Men

For the moderate packer, this is an eight- or nine-piece basic travel wardrobe. Use it for trips of any length between one week and one year, in varying climates, and for diverse activities. Men's clothing is large, so this wardrobe may be the most that you can pack in a carry-on bag. Limit the number of garments by selecting versatile styles in compact, packable fabrics.

The basic eight or nine garments:

- ▼ 1 suit *or* a jacket with coordinating slacks
- ▼ 1 or 2 additional pairs of slacks that coordinate with the jacket
- ▼ 2 short-sleeved shirts
- ▼ 2 long-sleeved shirts
- ▼ 1 dark, thin-knit, medium-weight sweater

A SAMPLE PACKING LIST—MEN'S MODERATE WARDROBE

Here is a sample packing list for a moderate wardrobe, organized by layer:

Layer 1 – Underlayer

- ▼ 2 T-shirts (1 extra-large for cover-up or sleepwear, or add pajamas)
- ▼ Silk or polyester thermal underwear (for cold weather; this can double as sleepwear)
- ▼ 2-8 sets undershorts, depending on how frequently you plan to wash them

- ▼ 2-4 undershirts, if desired
- ▼ 1 pair of swim trunks

Layer 2 – Clothing

- ▼ 1 jacket and 1 pair of slacks *or* 1 suit
- ▼ 2 pairs of slacks for day or evening
- ▼ 4 shirts, at least 2 long-sleeved
- ▼ 1 pullover sweater (V-neck is the most versatile)
- ▼ 1 pair of shorts (optional)
- ▼ Athletic clothing and underwear, if needed

Layer 3 – Outerlayer/Raingear

- ▼ 1 raincoat *or* rainjacket

Layer 4 – Extremities

- ▼ 2-7 pairs of dress socks
- ▼ 2-7 pairs of athletic socks (thin and medium-weight, drip-dry)
- ▼ 1 pair of walking or athletic shoes
- ▼ 1 pair of dress shoes
- ▼ 1 pair of sandals or thongs
- ▼ Sun hat, rain hat
- ▼ Gloves, if needed

Accessories

- ▼ 1 belt
- ▼ 1 or 2 ties
- ▼ Cufflinks and handkerchiefs, if needed
- ▼ Umbrella

The Minimalist Wardrobe for Men

The minimalist travel wardrobe is perfect for short or single-purpose (for example, business or casual) trips. You will be washing fairly often. Vary the sleeve lengths according to climate and style.

The basic six garments:

▼ 1 suit *or* 1 sport jacket with 1 pair coordinating slacks in a neutral color *or* 1 medium-weight V-neck or crew neck sweater with coordinating slacks (you may not need a jacket for a casual trip—a sweater and your rainwear may be sufficient)

▼ 1 additional pair of pants that coordinate with the suit or jacket

▼ 2 long-sleeved shirts

▼ 1 short-sleeved shirt (polo-type knit shirts are versatile)

To make a packing list, follow the list above for the moderate wardrobe, substituting your six garments as Layer 2. Add a pair of shorts if you want.

The Luxury Wardrobe for Men

You will need a second bag or a suit bag for the luxury wardrobe. Add to the moderate wardrobe *one* of the following outfits:

▼ 1 suit *or*

▼ 1 jacket and a pair of slacks *or*

▼ 1 sweater and a pair of slacks *or*

▼ 1 special-event outfit

▼ A Trip to Europe

A two- or three-week trip to Europe involves visits to big cities, side-trips to country villages, perhaps a beach resort, and religious sites. Probablility of rain is often likely. In the city, you want to be stylishly casual during the day, with an occasional dressy look for evenings. Long sightseeing days require clothing that can transition easily from day into evening. Yet you will also need comfortable, casual clothing for day hikes, dress-down days, and the beach. Layer versatile, simple separates that are very comfortable. Solid colors are best. Black and white with an added bright color is a versatile color combination. Important accessories: a daybag large enough to contain a change of shoes, skirt or blouse, scarf, and jewelry for quick changes, plus a raincoat and umbrella. Also, don't forget to wear your security wallet at all times.

Note: If your style is more casual, take all casual items and one dress-up outfit, or see the Adventure Wardrobe (see pp. 149–152). To travel extra light, take only three bottom pieces. For summer heat take SuppleX nylon, cotton, cotton blends, and linen; for winter cold take midweight wool and wool blends. Make sure your shoes are comfortable!

European Travel Wardrobe for Women

Citywear

- ▼ 1 jacket (loose blazer type)
- ▼ 1 cardigan sweater
- ▼ 1 pair of casual slacks
- ▼ 1 pair of nice slacks
- ▼ 1 simple skirt
- ▼ 2 T-shirts (my favorite is jewelneck for versatility)
- ▼ 2 blouses (1 slightly dressy one to go with nice slacks)
- ▼ 1 slightly dressy two-piece dress, simple dress, jumper, or skirt and blouse
- ▼ 1 pair of dress shoes
- ▼ 1 pair of walking shoes
- ▼ 1 extra large T-shirt for cover-up, sleepwear; or nightgown/pajamas
- ▼ 2-3 pairs of socks (4-5 for winter)
- ▼ 2-3 pairs of hose or tights (prewash to minimize runs)
- ▼ 4-5 pairs of underwear
- ▼ 2 bras/garment shields
- ▼ 1 scarf (a sash can double as a head cover or belt)
- ▼ Jewelry (1 pair earrings you can sleep in; 1 nice pair for evening; plus simple pieces)
- ▼ 1 small purse for evening

Beachwear

- ▼ 1 swimsuit
- ▼ 1 pair of shorts (khaki walking shorts or knit pull-ons)

- ▼ 1 T-shirt or tank top (try to match with the skirts for additional versatility)
- ▼ 1 pair of thongs or sandals
- ▼ 1 sun hat

Travel gear essentials: security wallet, Packtowl, fold-up totebag for beach and wardrobe changes, picnic kit, packable raincoat, and umbrella.

European Travel Wardrobe for Men

Citywear

- ▼ 1 jacket (blazer, casual, or rainjacket)
- ▼ 1 sweater (medium-weight, thin knit)
- ▼ 1 pair of comfortable, casual pants
- ▼ 1 pair of all-purpose dressier slacks (i.e., khakis)
- ▼ 1 pair of walking shorts *or* 1 more pair of casual slacks (light-weight)
- ▼ 2 polo-type knit shirts
- ▼ 2 long-sleeved shirts (at least 1 white)
- ▼ Tie(s)
- ▼ 1 pair of walking shoes
- ▼ 1 pair of dress shoes (optional if walking shoes are all-purpose)
- ▼ 1 extra-large T-shirt for cover up, sleepwear; or p.j.'s
- ▼ 4-5 pairs of socks
- ▼ 4-5 pairs of underwear
- ▼ Belt
- ▼ 1 packable raincoat/umbrella if rain is expected

Beachwear

- ▼ 1 pair of swim trunks
- ▼ 1 T-shirt
- ▼ Sun hat
- ▼ Thongs or sandals

Travel gear essentials: security wallet, Packtowl, expandable tote, picnic kit, packable rainjacket or raincoat, and umbrella.

▼ Beach/Resort/Cruise Wardrobe

Hawaii, the Caribbean, Mexico, here we come—sunshine by day, partying by night. Prepared with a simple mix and match wardrobe, you don't have to overpack.

On a cruise, there are plenty of opportunities to shop on the ship and in port so it is almost impossible to be without a necessity. A basic wardrobe of lightweight shorts and tops for the day, a few nice casual outfits, and a couple of compact evening outfits (see Tilley Endurables, p. 198) or a tuxedo is the framework for your "traveling light" packing plan. You'll probably need a garment bag, though.

Important cruising gear includes a daypack or tote stocked with a change of clothes and personal items, since your luggage may take awhile to get to your cabin; bathing suits and a nice cover-up for the pool areas (a pareo is great here); security wallet and phrasebook for shore excursions, antacid and elastic waistbands to compensate for the midnight buffets, hat, water bottle, sun-protective sunscreen, shirt, and insect repellent for warm weather or tropical cruising. An umbrella and windbreaker, and workoutwear for the gym will also come in handy, as will a nightlight for the cabin. For Alaska and adventure cruising, any weather is possible. See Cold-Weather Travel for packing tips, pp. 152–153. Make sure to bring your binoculars! For tropical weather, see pp. 153–155.

If a resort is your destination, your main consideration will be regarding specific dress codes. You also need to think about packing sports equipment. If it is at all possible, try renting equipment once you arrive so you don't have to lug it. Call ahead to find out what people wear on the tennis courts and in the restaurant, and pack accordingly.

For beach trips, include a Packtowl instead of a cotton terry-cloth towel, and a waterproof security wallet (see pp. 36–39).

Women

- ▼ 1 sweater
- ▼ 1 cotton skirt or culottes

- ▼ 1 pair of lightweight pants
- ▼ 1 pair of leggings
- ▼ 2 pairs of shorts
- ▼ 1 jumper or sleeveless shift
- ▼ 3 T-shirts (vary the styles—jewelneck, tanks, three-quarter–sleeve)
- ▼ 1 lightweight long-sleeved shirt for sun protection
- ▼ 1-2 compact evening outfits
- ▼ 2 bathing suits
- ▼ pareo or attractive cover-up
- ▼ 1 shawl or sash scarf
- ▼ 1 windbreaker/windpants
- ▼ Cotton socks, hosiery
- ▼ 1 pair of walking shoes
- ▼ 1 pair of sandals
- ▼ 1 pair of evening shoes
- ▼ Sport clothing and equipment

Men

- ▼ Sweater
- ▼ 2 pairs of lightweight slacks
- ▼ 1 pair shorts
- ▼ 2 button-down short-sleeved shirts
- ▼ 2 knit shirts-polo type
- ▼ 1 pair of swim trunks
- ▼ Pajamas or extra-large T-shirt for sleep
- ▼ Windbreaker
- ▼ (optional) Blazer/shirt/several ties
- ▼ 1 pair walking shoes
- ▼ 1 pair sandals
- ▼ 1 pair dress shoes and socks
- ▼ Sport clothing and equipment

For cruises add:

- ▼ 1 tuxedo or compact evening outfit, 1 sport jacket, slacks, shirt, and several ties

▼ Weekend Getaway Wardrobe

For this casual three- or four-day trip, you don't need much!

- ▼ 1 casual jacket
- ▼ 1 sweater (pullover or cardigan) or a vest
- ▼ 1 skirt
- ▼ 1 pair of pants
- ▼ 1 pair of shorts
- ▼ 1 blouse
- ▼ 2 T-shirts (one extra-large for nightshirt or swim cover-up)
- ▼ Bathing suit
- ▼ Sneakers or other comfortable shoes
- ▼ Comfortable flats or pumps
- ▼ 3-4 pairs of light- and medium weight socks
- ▼ 3-4 pairs of underwear

For cold weather adjustments, see p. 152.

▼ Adventure Travel

Bags packed for physically active vacations or trips to non-Western countries are far more likely to contain stuff taken "just in case" than are those packed for business travel, when the agenda is set in advance and amenities are readily available. Packing for an adventure trip or active vacation requires you to balance self-sufficiency against the need to travel light. The need for self-sufficiency increases if you travel in areas where such things as medications and clean water are not available. Also, you must be prepared for various microclimates (such as those of jungle basins or mountaintops) during a single trip. Then, if your itinerary includes visits to cities, you will need "civilized" clothing as well, taking into account local dress codes.

Below is the Basic Adventure Wardrobe with weather adjustments for cold, trekking/high altitude, wet/humid, and dry/desert climates. Fast-drying, high-performance clothing is mandatory, since active vacations bring one face-to-face with the elements and produce lots of laundry, too. A basic travel gear checklist is also included.

▼ Women's Basic Adventure Wardrobe

This wardrobe is suitable for any warm-weather, on-your-own trip, such as a trip to Asia. If cool weather is expected, select heavier fabrics and follow the suggestions in Adjusting for Weather (starting on p. 152).

MINIMALIST

Layer 1 – Under layer

- ▼ 2 or 3 T-shirts
- ▼ 4 pairs of underpants
- ▼ 2 bras
- ▼ 1 pareo, sarong, or large T-shirt (for sleeping, lounging, and cover-up)
- ▼ 1 bathing suit (one-piece)

Layer 2 – Clothing

- ▼ 1 lightweight cardigan
- ▼ 2 long-sleeved shirts
- ▼ 1 pair of slacks (cool, comfortable, loose-fitting; often sold as "hiking pants")
- ▼ 2 travel skirts, mid-length, lightweight cotton or cotton/synthetic blend with pockets
- ▼ 1 pair of walking shorts, knee-length, with pockets

Layer 3 – Outerlayer

- ▼ 1 lightweight raincoat, nylon poncho, or windbreaker, with hood

Layer 4 – Extremities

- ▼ 1 pair of walking shoes—these can be running shoes or lightweight walking shoes, which can be worn around camp, walking in the rainforest and in the city; or sturdy walking sandals. If you want a closed shoe for hiking in jungles or rivers, you will need a second pair of walking shoes that can get wet
- ▼ 1 pair of sturdy sandals—these can be "super sandals," such as Tevas, if you plan to be in rivers, reefs, beaches, or other wet places; otherwise, Clark's orthopedic sandals are great
- ▼ 1 pair of canvas shoes (espadrilles) *or* light sandals for dress (optional)
- ▼ 4 pairs of light- or medium weight socks, fast drying
- ▼ 4 pairs of lightweight socks (such as sock liners) in polyester (e.g. Capilene) or a silk knit
- ▼ 2 bandannas, 1 large for sun protection
- ▼ Hat—for sun, take a wide-brimmed style, preferably one that will protect your neck and ears; a baseball cap is also fine; be sure to use sunscreen

MODERATE

To the minimalist wardrobe add:

- ▼ 1 outfit for the city: short-sleeved camp shirt and skirt or a cool shirtdress
- ▼ 1 T-shirt
- ▼ Sashes, belts
- ▼ Jewelry, simple beads, and earrings
- ▼ 1 pair of espadrilles or sandals for the city

LUXURY

To the moderate wardrobe add:

▼ 1 outfit for the city

This will probably push you over the edge for one carry-on; avoid it if possible.

▼ Men's Basic Adventure Wardrobe

This wardrobe is suitable for any warm-weather trip. See guidelines for cool-weather changes, starting on p. 152.

MINIMALIST

Layer 1 – Underlayer

▼ 2 T-shirts (polo-style)

▼ 2-4 pairs of underpants (Coolmax is the best)

▼ 1 pair of swim trunks (shorts can double as trunks)

▼ 1 pareo, sarong, or large T-shirt (for sleeping, lounging, and cover-up)

Layer 2 – Clothing

▼ 1 lightweight sweater

▼ 2 long-sleeved shirts with pockets

▼ 2 pairs of slacks with pockets (cool, comfortable, loose-fitting trousers; those sold as "hiking pants," are good)

▼ 1 pair of walking shorts, knee-length, with pockets

Layer 3 – Outerlayer

▼ 1 lightweight nylon poncho or windbreaker, with hood

Layer 4 – Extremities

▼ 1 pair of walking shoes—these can be running shoes or lightweight walking shoes, which can be worn around camp, in town, and walking in the rainforest; if you want a closed shoe for hiking in jungles or rivers, you will need a second pair of walking shoes that can get wet

- ▼ 1 pair of sturdy sandals—these should be "super sandals," such as Tevas, if you plan to be in rivers, reefs, beaches, or other wet places; otherwise, any open, comfortable shoe is fine
- ▼ 4 pairs of fast drying, moisture wicking, lightweight socks
- ▼ 2 pairs of sock liners-Capilene
- ▼ 2 bandannas, 1 large
- ▼ Hat—for sun, take a wide-brimmed style, preferably one that will protect your neck and ears; a baseball cap is also fine; be sure to use sunscreen

MODERATE

To the minimalist wardrobe add:

- ▼ 1 jacket

LUXURY

To the moderate wardrobe add:

- ▼ 1 outfit for the city (slacks and shirt)

This will probably push you over the edge for one carry-on; avoid it if at all possible.

▼ Adjusting for Weather, Climate, and Type of Trip

You may need to adjust the fabrics, number of layers, and shoes depending on the conditions of your trip. Consider the following suggestions in selecting your adventure wardrobe.

Cold-Weather Travel

- ▼ Take warm wool or fleece socks and sock liners
- ▼ Add 2 pairs of underpants as they will dry more slowly
- ▼ Add thermal long underwear, cotton tights, or leggings
- ▼ Substitute a pair of heavier-weight slacks for the shorts
- ▼ Take a turtleneck instead of a T-shirt

- ▼ Substitute a wool or microfleece button-down long-sleeved shirt or pullover for the light long-sleeved shirt
- ▼ Substitute a fleece jacket for the cardigan
- ▼ Pack warm shoes instead of open shoes
- ▼ Add a warm hat and gloves

Trekking or Mountain Travel

If your trip includes a trek to high altitudes, add the following to the adventure wardrobe. Try to rent most equipment and heavy clothing at your destination.

- ▼ Long underwear (medium-weight)
- ▼ Anorak
- ▼ Down parka or vest (rent it at your destination if possible)
- ▼ Fleece jacket
- ▼ Waterproof raingear
- ▼ Lycra ski tights
- ▼ Lightweight weather-sealed hiking boots (do *not* rent these; wear them on the plane to save suitcase space)
- ▼ For the tropics, take ankle-height, nylon hiking boots with removable insoles, or light, weather-sealed leather boots
- ▼ 2 pairs of thick, quick-drying socks, and sock liners
- ▼ Wool or fleece hat
- ▼ Mittens or gloves (optional)
- ▼ Sneakers

Tropical Travel

Humidity, intense sun, periodic rain, and cold at high altitudes are marks of the tropics. You need high-performance outdoor gear that dries quickly. Sunscreen, lip balm, mosquito repellent and/or netting, and anti-itch remedies are essential.

For tropical travel, take the Adventure Wardrobe and follow these guidelines:

CLOTHING

Choose lightweight garments that will protect you from the sun and insects. Clothes should be loose-fitting in a weave that helps ventilate the body. T-shirts should be of 100 percent cotton or a cotton/polyester blend. Fast-drying rayon and other technical T's are available, too. Mesh polo-type T-shirts are good because they protect the neck from the sun and are more versatile than plain T-shirts are. Long-sleeved shirts can be of cotton/polyester blends. A combination of 55–65 percent cotton and 35–45 percent polyester makes a good fabric. Patagonia makes one called "Fishing Gear;" Ex Officio makes the "Baja Shirt" and the "Wayfarer." Patagonia also makes an "A/C" line of clothing especially for humid weather. Tarponwear and Railrides also have an excellent line. (See Resources for more information.)

Ideally, skirts, slacks, and sport jackets can be of easy-care fabrics made of Supplex nylon, polyester/cotton, cotton/nylon, or tropical weight wool/polyester blends. Spandex gives clothing an added measure of comfort. Women may want to bring a cool shirtdress for citywear. Underwear should be of quick-drying synthetics or synthetic blends such as Coolmax. Shorts are not acceptable in all areas—check before packing them. You may want to consider a conservative, knee-length style with lots of pockets in a quick-drying cotton/nylon blend. Take a sun hat and chiffon scarves or bandannas to keep the sun off your head. If you have time to shop, hats, scarves, and sarongs will often be available at your destination. Plan on washing one item while the second dries, and buy everything in fast-drying fabrics. Excellent manufacturers are Ex Officio, Sierra Designs, Travelsmith, Royal Robbins, Tarponwear, Railriders, and Early Winters.

Note: In Asia and Moslem countries, women's wardrobes should be modest.

SHOES

In humid climates, shoes will get very sweaty and heavy. Mildew is a constant threat. It may be slightly harder to consolidate and wear the same shoes all the time. Try to limit yourself to three pairs of shoes.

If you are going to be in wet places such as rivers, jungles, beaches, and caves, take a pair of "super sandals", such as Tevas, which provide excellent support and remain comfortable when wet.

Take a walking shoe with a removable insole, choosing a light-weight, open-weave model. For the tropics, avoid leather because it is too heavy and does not dry.

The second pair should be a sturdy, comfortable sandal or walking shoe. For this you could use your Tevas or a supportive sandal such as those made by Clark's. You will wear these every day for traveling and walking. Women may want a lightweight pair of espadrilles or sandals for dress.

Desert Travel

Desert trips are characterized by dry, sunny weather with lots of wind, dust, and possible rain. The nights are cool. Desert gear should include a dustbag for your camera, eyedrops such as Visine for dust, Solarcaine if you burn, wide-brimmed cap or hat, one or two large bandannas for dust, spare sunglasses, and, if you wear contacts, extra eyewash, lens cleaner, and glasses or goggles to protect against dust.

If on safari, choose comfortable clothing for long days spent riding in vans. There probably won't be much city travel. Depending on your destination and the time of year, you may need extra layers for warmth or rain. Take the Basic Adventure Wardrobe, with the following changes:

▼ 2-4 T-shirts

▼ 2 long-sleeved shirts (1 light for sunny days; 1 warmer for cool evenings)

▼ 2 pairs of pants, 1 in cotton or cotton/polyester twill; 1 in lighter weight, such as cotton/nylon, cotton/polyester sheeting, or Supplex nylon

▼ Consider a warm fleece jacket or sweater for cold nights, and a windbreaker/rainjacket

Summer Hiking/Cycling/Hosteling Travel

Bring a super-light wardrobe for a summer of hosteling and hiking or cycling. For cycling, take cotton or Coolmax underwear, three pairs of socks, and substitute sturdy walking or cycling shoes for the hiking boots. If you want to dress up in the city, add one simple nice outfit. Take the Basic Adventure Wardrobe with the following changes:

- ▼ 1 long-sleeved shirt instead of 2
- ▼ 1 all-purpose wool or fleece sweater instead of a light cardigan
- ▼ 1 pair of slacks and 2 pairs of shorts (no skirts)
- ▼ Add 1 waterproof rainjacket and pants or poncho
- ▼ Add 2 pairs of hiking socks and 2 pairs of sock liners
- ▼ Substitute sturdy, comfortable hiking boots for walking shoes
- ▼ Add light sneakers for wearing around camp

▼ Gear for Adventure Travel

For details, see chapter 3.

- ☐ money pouch or belt for carrying valuables
- ☐ daypack with lock—for carrying cameras and lenses, water bottle, rain gear, and so on. Small pockets are useful for film, sun cream, and sunglasses. Look for padded shoulder straps and waistband. Line the pack with a heavy gauge-garbage bag in rainy weather.
- ☐ convertible pack; the zipper should lock. Line the pack with a heavy-gauge garbage bag in rainy weather
- ☐ expandable nylon totebag—for storing city clothes at the hotel or in a locker while in the field
- ☐ luggage locks and tags
- ☐ personal prescriptions, medications, antibiotics (if necessary)
- ☐ first-aid kit with small booklet, IAMAT doctors list (see Resources)
- ☐ malaria pills if needed, antidiarrheal and headache remedies
- ☐ iodine tablets or water purification equipment (see pp. 45–46)
- ☐ water bottle—a wide-mouth bottle is best if you plan to bring drink mixes
- ☐ pocket knife/compass/pocket mirror/tool kit/matches/tweezers
- ☐ tool kit

- [ ] sunglasses and retainer strap (get glasses that offer good UV protection)
- [ ] insect repellent; mosquito netting (headnet or other), if desired; mosquito itch-aid
- [ ] sunscreen or sunblock cream with a Sun Protection Factor (SPF) of 15 or higher
- [ ] lip sunblock with an SPF of 15 or higher (such as Chapstick 15, A-fil, or Labiosan)
- [ ] headlamp, Beam-and-Read light, or flashlight—for reading or writing in your journal at night. Take 2 sets of extra batteries and bulbs if you read at night.
- [ ] toilet paper—remove the cardboard tube
- [ ] Packtowl or a small, thin towel
- [ ] sewing kit
- [ ] bandanna
- [ ] travel umbrella
- [ ] travel alarm or watch with alarm
- [ ] journal, stationery, and pen
- [ ] toiletries kit; toothbrush and toothpaste; biodegradable shampoo and soap, deodorant, skin moisturizer, nail brush, nail clippers, small packages of Kleenex and Wash'n'Dris, razor, shaving cream, baby powder, laundry soap. Adequate supplies of sanitary items.
- [ ] spare eyeglasses and spare prescription sunglasses or clip-ons as a back-up; eyeglass straps. Contact lenses can be worn successfully, but be sure to bring a sufficient supply of solutions, including in-the-eye lubricants. An eyeglass repair kit is also handy.
- [ ] camera equipment—water resistant is best.

8

Traveling with Kids

You *can* go carry-on with kids! The strategy is three-fold: Choose luggage and equipment that enhances your mobility; make every person as self-sufficient as possible; and abandon the notion that you take everything with you. A few well-chosen garments, snacks, toys, books, and tapes will be all your family needs to keep going. Your best bet is to buy babies and small children a ticket. This guarantees them a seat and their carry-on luggage allotment. If this is not an option, check with your airlines about their carry-on regulations.

▼ Luggage

Choose a luggage and equipment configuration that will enable you to balance bags and kids as you negotiate airports, planes, and crowds. The convertible backpack/daypack system works best for parents and kids age six and older (between 3 feet, 6 inches and 5 feet, 2 inches tall). Kids can easily carry their own luggage on their backs or pull a kid's wheelaboard. Small children, between the ages of three and five, can pack a small duffel or a daypack with their belongings. Make sure it complements your luggage as you may end up carrying it.

Tough Traveler manufactures KidSYSTEMS, a full line of luggage, packs, child-carriers, and daypacks especially for children. Those between the ages of five and eleven can carry the versatile Mini-Van, a frameless convertible pack/suitcase. It's also a great smaller bag for adults! Held horizontally, it is a single-cavity suitcase. Turn it vertically, open the flap, and out comes a full padded waistband and set of shoulder straps. The Camper is an internal-frame pack that gives more support to the back. This model is excellent for walking and hiking as well as for all-purpose travel. Kids over the age of nine (between 4 feet, 6 inches and 5 feet, 6 inches tall) interested in an internal-frame pack suitable for all trips, including extensive hiking, will love The Ranger. Children eleven or older will enjoy The Caravan, a larger version of the Mini-Van frameless convertible pack/suitcase with lots of added outside pockets. At this age, depending on their size, kids can also wear adult 22-inch travel packs.

For a trip without a lot of luggage handling, Tough Traveler makes a 17.5-inch cordura nylon Kid's Flight Bag, a suitcase with handles and a shoulder strap that has three compartments for the convenient separation of clean and dirty clothes, and books and toys.

Tutto makes the colorful "Gizmo" line of kids' luggage and daypacks. My kids each have one and they are great! The 20-inch, 4-wheeled suitcase pulls or pushes along easily with a U-shaped pullbar and can also be used as a seat or loaded with other extras (like my daughter Sara's dolls). All the luggage pieces feature reflective tape on the outside. The external frame is incredibly sturdy and the bag collapses to $2\frac{1}{2}$ inches for easy under-the-bed storage. Two-wheeled rollaboards for kids are also appearing in the marketplace, but none with the adult quality of Tutto's wheeled bags or KidSYSTEMS travel packs.

When traveling with babies and small children, parents will find that the convertible pack enables them to travel hands-free to hold the children and a car seat, or to push a stroller. A baby front- or side-carrier can be worn at the same time. Or one parent might wear the child in a backpack-type child carrier while carrying a suitcase that has a shoulder strap or towing a wheeled bag. An additional umbrella stroller may be added if you have several small children. If necessary, a sturdy luggage cart, such as the Remin Concorde III, will carry numerous bags easily.

Take an expandable nylon suitcase that folds up in a small pouch. You will find a hundred purposes for this bag. The best one is that, if your carry-on allotment is limited, you can pack your baby's belongings in your own luggage and then whisk out the tote and transfer baby's gear while settling in for your flight.

All children, including infants, require a passport for foreign travel. Keep passports, money, traveler's checks, and tickets in a security wallet worn underneath your clothing. Two parents can divide multiple passports between them. A parent traveling alone with several children should wear two wallets to store valuables. Include prescription photocopies for medicine (for yourself and for your child), copies of your child's medical information, and the number of your pediatrician and health insurance plan on your address list. (The checklist on pp. 39–40 details the items that should be safeguarded in your security wallet.)

Instead of carrying a big purse, keep a small change purse or a nylon zip bag or wallet in the diaper bag for access to cash. A fanny pack will also work (but do not use it for valuables).

▼ Self-Sufficiency

Make each family member as self-sufficient as possible. This increases a child's sense of participation and lessens the burden on parents. Let kids pack their own daypack with a light jacket or sweatshirt, bottle or cup of juice, snack, and a few favorite books, toys, tapes, and a personal tape player. One parent can keep a backup stock of food in his or her luggage or a soft insulated cooler bag with a shoulder strap. A fanny pack is also useful, especially if the child is already carrying their backpack. Make sure to pack a lightweight daypack in the suitcase, though, for day hikes and excursions.

▼ Food

Hungry children are no fun on the road. Make sure each child is equipped with a water bottle and snacks. Apples, grapes, and other fruit that does not drip or stain, dried fruit, crackers, cereal or bagels, granola bars, trail mix, and cheese-and-cracker packs are good choices. Get kids into the habit of drinking plain water when they are thirsty and you eliminate the constant need to buy or deal with juices that can stain clothes.

Bottle-fed babies should have enough for regular feedings and for two more meals in case you get delayed. Toddlers and small children should have finger foods in sandwich bags. Consider bringing a bag lunch on the flight if your child is a picky eater. Food may not always be available at baby's feeding times and toddlers may not like what is served. (You can request "baby" and "toddler" meals from the airline in advance.) Juice and water are usually available on the flight.

Takeoff and landing are good times to give children a bottle, or let them nurse or eat a snack. This will help alleviate possible ear pain caused by changes in air pressure. Or, use Children's Earplanes (see Special Accessories for Kids p. 167).

▼ Entertainment

Choose items carefully for their portability and value. Simple items that rely on children's creativity, manipulation, and imagination will outlast items that stimulate superficially. I find that books and story cassette tape sets are the best form of entertainment (after Mom and Dad, that is). You can buy and trade books along the way, and have them sent to you during a long trip. Make sure to bring a book with the words to songs, activities, and fingerplay. Below I list several practical and entertaining items for each age group.

Babies

- ▼ 2 or 3 board books (vinyl are especially light)
- ▼ Rattles, especially those with moving parts, or dangling things such as plastic keys or measuring spoons
- ▼ A soft cloth ball
- ▼ Teethers (such as a toothbrush)
- ▼ Nesting objects
- ▼ Mirror (use your pocket mirror)

Toddlers

- ▼ A "Bag of Tricks"—a purse or sandwich bag with odd things they are not normally allowed to play with, or a plastic seven-day pill dispenser filled with raisins and cereal (the child will be busy for hours opening and closing the caps)
- ▼ Picture books and cassette tapes

- ▼ A book of songs such as *Wee Sing* so a parent can sing to them
- ▼ Finger puppets
- ▼ A favorite doll with a doll-sized blanket
- ▼ Art materials: crayons and paper; a small paintbrush and "Paint with Water" coloring books
- ▼ Duplos

Small Children (Over Three Years Old)

- ▼ Storybooks with cassettes to be used with a walkman or headphones (my son listened to *Sleeping Beauty* for three straight hours in the car)
- ▼ Art materials: paper and paper bags, string, pipe cleaners, blunt scissors to practice cutting, Scotch tape, crayons, chalk, a paintbrush and a "Paint with Water" book, dot-to-dot books
- ▼ An erasable travel slate (look for the lighter cardboard type)
- ▼ Portable dolls and play figures
- ▼ Legos
- ▼ A tennis ball
- ▼ Small cars or a small pouch of micro-cars
- ▼ A small, divided plastic pill box useful for collecting small things, which kids love to do

Older Children

- ▼ Walkman with tapes and headphones, or a microcassette recorder for recording stories, chronicling the trip, and so on
- ▼ Books; a tiny atlas
- ▼ Art materials: paper, scissors, tape or gluestick, sketch pad, colored pencils, sharpener
- ▼ Journal and pens
- ▼ Small cars
- ▼ Small travel games (magnetic checkers, electronic games, etc.)
- ▼ Cards (get a small book of card games so you can play all kinds)

- ▼ Camera and film
- ▼ Crafts (for example, string and beads for making necklaces, needlepoint, crocheting, and so on)

▼ Clothing

Use the rules for grown-ups when packing for kids.

- ▼ Pack as minimally as possible, taking into account your laundry schedule. Try the "wash-one/wear-one" strategy, plus minimal backup. If you wish to do laundry only once a week, you will need to add clothing.
- ▼ Choose a color scheme for mix and match. All pieces should coordinate. This makes it easier for kids to dress themselves.
- ▼ Pay *extra* attention to layering. Babies and kids are especially at risk in cold weather. Each item of clothing should function as part of a layering system, complete with a moisture-wicking inner layer, insulating layer(s), and an outer layer. Do not forget to protect the extremities with hats, gloves, mittens, balaclavas, and so on.
- ▼ Pack separates—they are more versatile and layer easily. They also make diaper changing easier. Add a couple of sleepers for infants.
- ▼ Choose easy-care, fast-drying fabrics in various light and medium weights. Denim should be limited to soft, lightweight overalls that dry quickly.
- ▼ Choose dark colors and prints whenever possible—these conceal stains (this goes for the parents of small kids, too).

Packing Tips

Older kids and teenagers can use the Bundle Method. Put a packing list in their luggage for repacking so that they will not forget anything.

For smaller kids, roll outfits together so they can easily unpack and dress themselves. (If everything is color-coordinated, any choice they make will be presentable.) You can put rubber bands around the bundles or put them in plastic bags, if you like.

Keep the nice outfit (including shoes, socks, and hair accessories) in a plastic bag or stuff sack.

Set aside one play outfit (such as sturdy overalls) for getting really dirty—the rest should then remain relatively clean.

Appoint one person to carry all the swimsuits in a stuff sack, another the pajamas, and so on. This will speed up unpacking.

Clothing for unticketed babies and toddlers may have to go in a parent's suitcase. Lay the clothes neatly on top of the bundle or in one section of your suitcase.

Laundry

Each person can carry their own soiled clothing in a stuff sack. A laundry bag is convenient for car travel. I like the Over-the-Door Neat Net (available at Toys R Us), a large nylon mesh hamper with two hooks that hangs up out of the way. The expandable nylon tote also makes a good hamper.

To prevent stains, ban popsicles, powdered drink mixes, and gelatin desserts, which contain dye; mustard; and dark red fruits and fruit juices from your menu. Carry a pretreat spot-and-stain-remover stick along with a flask of water to prevent stains from setting until you can launder them. (For a laundry checklist, see pp. 218–219.)

Hint: Take a one-ounce bottle of white vinegar—it will treat tomato (i.e., pizza and spaghetti sauce) stains. For more on stains, see pp. 222–226.

Layering Strategies for Children

Because of their small size and activity habits, children are more at risk for cold than adults are. Patagonia, a clothing company that makes functional layering pieces for babies, children, and adults offers this advice.

BABIES AND TODDLERS

Babies have less insulating fat than older children have. They are also fairly sedentary, being carried in a pack or stroller. Dress babies and toddlers up to two years old in warm thin layers with a hat and, because they cannot communicate discomfort verbally, look often for signs of cold or overheating. Feel their extremities—ears, nose, fingers, and toes. Fleece bunting bags are ideal.

THREE- TO SIX-YEAR-OLDS

Little kids may be so busy playing that their sensations go unnoticed. They need a wicking layer and clothing that is easily put on and taken off. Jackets and pants need to have growing room with no loss of insulation.

KIDS OVER SIX

Kids need a wicking layer along with insulation and a shell that they can easily manipulate as temperatures and exertion vary. Do not let a child's enthusiasm exceed his common sense. Children often want to keep on playing rather than come indoors just because they are cold.

OLDER KIDS

Older kids want the function and style of adult gear. They are able to use technical features. They're old enough to understand the potential warning signs and dangers of cold and can easily use a layering system.

PROTECT THE EXTREMITIES

Over half the body heat a child produces can be lost through the head. In cold or wet weather, always cover a young child's head and neck with a hat or insulating hood. Protect their faces with scarves, balaclavas, and neck gaiters in windy weather. Gloves can be worn under mittens. Two pairs of socks add warmth (make sure shoes or boots are sized to accommodate them).

▼ A Child's Travel Wardrobe

This wardrobe will do for children of all ages. Note additions for infants.

MINIMALIST

Layer 1 – Underlayer
- ▼ 3 T-shirts (1 extra-large for pool or beach cover-up)
- ▼ 5–8 pairs of underpants

- ▼ 1 pair of tights or leggings
- ▼ 1 swimsuit
- ▼ 1 pair of pajamas—a fleece-type blanket sleeper replaces blankets

For babies add:

- ▼ 1 or 2 sleepers
- ▼ 2 onesies (T-shirts that snap at the crotch)

Layer 2 – Clothing

- ▼ 2 long-sleeved shirts (1 light)
- ▼ 2 or 3 long pants or overalls (1 can be sweatpants if cool weather is expected)
- ▼ 2 pairs of shorts or skirts (or 1 of each)
- ▼ 1 sweatshirt with a hood *or* a thin, warm sweater
- ▼ 1 nice outfit, if needed

Layer 3 – Outerlayer

- ▼ Packable rainjacket with hood

Layer 4 – Extremities

- ▼ 5 pairs of socks *or* 2 pairs of infant booties
- ▼ 1 pair of sneakers
- ▼ 1 pair of sandals or thongs
- ▼ 1 pair of dress shoes, if needed
- ▼ Sun hat with a wide brim, a means of tying it in the wind (chin tie, elasticized headband); ear and neck flaps are good too—try those made by Flap Happy.

For cold-weather travel add:

- ▼ Silk or polyester knit long underwear, top and bottom
- ▼ 3 pairs of thin socks for sock liners
- ▼ A fleece baby bag, vest, or jacket
- ▼ An appropriate outershell
- ▼ Glove liners, mittens
- ▼ A wool or fleece hat, with ear flaps

Special Accessories for Kids

▼ Children's Earplanes—These disposable earplug-like devices are for children ages 5–12 who suffer from ear discomfort during takeoff and landing, either due to cold, allergies and sinus conditions, or just "because." An adult version is also available for ages 12 and up.

▼ I.D. bracelet—This all-important device helps locate lost children. Write or tape the child's name, current hotel, and phone number to the underside. If traveling abroad, also indicate "U.S. Embassy". (See Resources.)

▼ Packtowl—Packtowls are invaluable for sponging, mopping, wiping, and so on. Buy at least one, cut one-third of it into small washcloths, and use the other two-thirds as a towel or mop-up cloth.

▼ Travel pillow—You can find baby-sized travel pillows at Toys R Us. Inflatable pillows are available from Easy Going and other stores.

▼ Nightlight—Do not forget one of these for unfamiliar hotel rooms. You need a converter and adapter for foreign destinations. Lightsticks are a good alternative.

▼ Hamper—Over-the-Door Neat Net is a mesh laundry bag perfect for fixed-base trips because it hangs up out of the way and is very lightweight. Available at Toys R Us.

▼ Equipment for Babies and Small Children

To go carry-on you can take at most a car seat and/or (depending on the airline) a portable umbrella stroller or a child-carrier onto the plane. Arrange, rent, or borrow cribs and other equipment in advance.

Car Seat

If you will be driving, you will need an FAA-approved car seat (they are labeled accordingly). This will also provide a comfortable place for the baby to eat and sleep. Some car rental agencies rent car seats, too. A revolutionary alternative for babies that weigh over 25 pounds is the

FAA-approved Travel Vest by AOK, a packable 5-point harness that may be attached to a car or airline seat belt. (See Lullaby Lane in Resources.)

If the flight is not full (call ahead), it pays to bring the car seat with you to the gate. If there is room, they will seat you next to an empty seat; if the plane is full, the crew will stow or check the car seat. You can always ask them to keep it inside the cabin; they may oblige.

Umbrella Stroller

If you will be driving and your sightseeing stops are accessible to strollers (some museums do not allow them), take a compact umbrella stroller with small, sturdy, easily maneuvered double wheels. Make sure that it collapses easily and can be carried with one hand.

Backpack Child Carriers

Carrying a child on your back is ideal if you will be taking public transportation, hiking, or walking on terrain where strollers are not convenient. Backpack carriers also provide freer access for the parent maneuvering in crowds, stores, and other public places. A small child can remain in a backpack carrier all day, resting, sightseeing, and sleeping at will. Tough Traveler manufactures frame child carriers for kids between the ages of six months (when they can sit up with their heads unsupported) and four years. These carriers collapse and are easily stowed in the overhead bin. Gerry Products also makes a good line of child carriers.

When choosing a child carrier, consider its primary use and your comfort as well as baby's. If the pack will be baby's sole mode of transportation with lots of all-day hiking and walking (and baby sleeping), Tough Traveler's highly technical Kid Carrier will be most comfortable for parent and child. It takes loads of up to 50 pounds and fits parents between 5 feet, 1 inch and 6 feet, 4 inches tall. The carrier has fully padded straps and waistbands, back ventilation, and lots of control straps to distribute the load. The even more elaborate Filly assures long-range comfort (all-day and longer hiking) when carrying loads of up to 60 pounds. This one is appropriate for giving older kids a respite. For a simpler, less expensive pack ideal for local trips and short hikes, the Montana still offers parents control straps and a sternum (chest) strap to fine-tune the load.

All packs have a large pouch under the seat for storing diapers, gear, and snacks. Optional equipment includes a rain or sun hood, stirrups, and on the Kid Carrier, a side pocket set.

Take a small pocket mirror along so that you can see your child, and make sure she's wearing her hat.

Soft Carriers for Infants

Soft infant carriers are convenient for holding infants between birth and nine months of age on the parent's body in a hands-free mode. Easily stowed, they are ideal for travel. Tummy packs such as those made by Gerry, Tough Traveler, and many other companies, handle babies up to nine months of age. Choose one that supports the baby's head and allows baby to see out. A quick-drying fabric is an advantage. Sara's Ride is a soft carrier designed for infants able to sit up; the child rides sitting on the parent's lap.

Harnesses

Harnesses are quite helpful for keeping tabs on wandering toddlers in crowded airports and train stations when you have a great deal of luggage. Harnesses also eliminate the need for a playpen. Be careful not to let the child get tangled up.

A Place to Sleep

Portable cribs have no place as carry-on luggage; consider other sleeping arrangements.

For babies that cannot crawl yet:

▼ Use your blanket to line a drawer for baby to sleep in.

▼ Baby Bjorn makes an inflatable changing cushion with sides; this will do for a baby who cannot climb out.

▼ Make a small bedroll: Cut a piece of insulite bought from a camping store and cover it with a large rubberized protector pad and a small sheet. Roll everything up and strap it to the bottom of your travel pack.

For crawlers and toddlers:

▼ Pack a small, inflatable pool that you can lay on the floor and line with a blanket or pad.

- ▼ The Right Start Catalog offers the Traveln'Trundle travel bed that rolls up into a stiff sack. It weighs three pounds and measures $48 \times 22^{1}/_{2} \times 4^{1}/_{2}$ inches high. Call (800) 548-8531 to order.

- ▼ Transfer the child onto a child-sized sleeping pad (such as EVA blue foam or Therm-a-Rest, which you can carry strapped to your luggage) after the child has fallen asleep on your bed.

- ▼ Push a bed against the wall and flank it with chairs to make sure the child cannot roll off.

Diapers

If you will be traveling where baby supplies are available, pack light. Bring enough trim, extra-absorbent diapers to get you to your destination. Be open minded about other brands if you cannot find the one you know. If you are going off the beaten path, take cloth diapers and wraps that you can wash and reuse as you go (read *Adventuring with Children* by Nan Jeffrey, Foghorn Press, 1992, for more on using cloth diapers). Pack a few extra diapers for emergencies.

▼ Packing Tips

I like to pack kits for kids—a diaper kit, a medical kit, a food kit. Invest in durable, zippered, nylon pouches. An insulated, foldable, six-pack bag with a shoulder strap is also handy.

The Diaper/Flight Bag

Let's assume you are allowed one bag for baby and/or toddler. The best investment is the Deluxe Diaper Bag (measuring $16 \times 9 \times 11$ inches; $45) made by Land's End (see Resources). This sturdy, high-capacity bag accommodates diapers, wipes, several changes of clothes, books and toys, four bottles or cups in insulated pockets, and between four and eight jars of baby food. It comes with a zippered foldable pouch for baby's toiletries (I use this to make the diaper kit), a removable zippered pouch for wet and soiled items, a compact changing pad, and a front pocket for the parent's stuff.

Any large daypack or tote will also serve this purpose, especially if you also have an insulated six-pack, lunch, or bottle bag for bottles and food. The diaper/flight bag should contain:

A DIAPER KIT

A small diaper kit is incredibly handy. It can be passed back and forth between parents. After changing baby, restock the bag immediately for your next use. Use any easily identifiable zippered nylon pouch measuring about 7 × 12 inches.

The kit itself consists of 1 diaper, 1 pack of wipes (a travel-sized package or a Ziploc bag filled with wet wipes), 1 rubberized lap pad, 1 compact vinyl changing pad, 1 small tube of diaper rash cream, and 2 plastic bags for soiled diapers.

EXTRA DIAPERS

The remainder of your diaper supply (enough for the first leg of your trip) should be distributed in your suitcases, tucked into corners, or lining edges. You can also use your expandable nylon tote for diapers, and stow it away as they are used up.

▼ Resealable plastic bags in quart and gallon sizes, or a roll of sandwich bags

▼ Baby wipes—Take them out of the original container and place them in a resealable plastic bag.

▼ 2 wet Packtowl washcloths in separate resealable plastic bags—1 for washing hands and faces, 1 as a mop-up cloth for tables, chairs, and so on

▼ Nursing pads

If needed:

▼ 2 all-purpose burp or nursing–cover-up cloths—use thin gauze-type cloth diapers or Packtowl or thin flannel receiving blanket (these dry fast).

▼ Waterproof dropcloth—Disposable Lammies or a 1-yard-square of vinyl to be used for protecting beds, too

▼ Toiletry kit—Small bottles of liquid baby soap, which doubles as soap and shampoo, powder if used, baby sunscreen, toothbrush, and baby nail clipper

- ▼ Pretreat stain and soil remover—Along with cold water, this is good for preventing stains from setting on washables.

COMFORT OBJECTS

- ▼ Pacifier, favorite toy, blanket
- ▼ Toys and books, a few old, a few new
- ▼ All-purpose blanket—One compact blanket for baby to play or sleep on, or for use as a nursing cover-up. This can also be a tablecloth for picnics or used to create a play area for all kids. I use a thinly quilted cotton/polyester style.

CLOTHING

- ▼ 2 outfits, including one for arrival. Pack comfortable, nonbinding separates. Include booties if baby is barefoot.
- ▼ 1 lightweight sweatshirt or nylon jacket with hood
- ▼ Sun hat

FOOD

This can be consolidated in the diaper bag or carried separately in an insulated cooler bag.

- ▼ Plenty of moist towelettes
- ▼ Finger food—dry cereal, crackers, bagels for baby and older children; cheese-and-cracker packs, fruit leather, raisins for older children
- ▼ Baby food—dehydrated, 3-ounce jars, or ready-to-serve microwave meals for babies older than 5 months
- ▼ A small plastic bowl with lid
- ▼ Spoons—2 sturdy plastic spoons (put long feeding spoons in a toothbrush container)
- ▼ Bib—laminated or pack of disposables (Lammies)
- ▼ Bottles—one for juice or water and one for formula, or take disposable liners; nipples, rings, and caps (1st Years makes a nipple

adapter so that you can fit any nipple on disposable-liner bottles.)

▼ Formula—ready-to-feed and dry, in a Ziploc bag. One method is to fill a 1-cup plastic container with powder and scoop. Keep the container and a bottle filled with water in the food bag to mix when needed. Replenish after use. Maya makes a pre-measured, 3-feedings cup. Use a pack that you preheat and wrap around the bottle to keep fluids warm.

▼ A spill-proof travel cup (if appropriate)

MEDICAL KIT

Add the following items to your own first-aid kit (see pp. 48–49) or put them in a place where baby cannot get to them.

▼ Phone number of your pediatrician, and IAMAT phone number (see Resources)

▼ Prescription medications and vitamins for baby (try to get those that do not need refrigeration)

▼ Syrup of Ipecac for accidental poisonings (administer only with medical advice)

▼ Medicine dispenser

▼ Thermometer (preferably nonmercury type for air trips)

▼ Baby acetaminophen

▼ Antidiarrheal medication (ask your doctor)

▼ Children's decongestant

▼ Insect repellent (low dose (17.5%) Deet for kids) and an anti-sting or itch treatment, such as calamine lotion, Benadryl, or 1% hydrocortisone cream

▼ Earplanes

▼ Safety outlet plugs

9

Packing for Teens

Why a separate chapter for teenagers? There are two reasons. One, teens are very fashion-conscious and tend to overpack. Two, they underestimate the necessity of protecting their valuables.

Experienced teen travelers know that traveling light is the way to go. Forget that big suitcase! Get a convertible backpack with a detachable daypack (see p. 22), use the Bundle Method outlined in chapter 5, and you will be set to go to camp, Europe, or any study program for weeks or months.

If you love fashion, here is your challenge: Create the greatest number of outfits possible from the fewest pieces of clothing, using layering principles along the way. Start early and refine your wardrobe before the trip. Then pack it and walk a mile. If you cannot handle it easily, go home and start throwing items out.

Follow the wardrobe guidelines outlined in earlier chapters. Here are the key points:

If traveling abroad, choose clothing that is appropriate, in terms of culture and climate, for your destination. Ask your sponsoring hosts or others who have been there. Shorts, revealing clothing, and sports clothing, for example, are not acceptable in many locales. Skirts may be more appropriate than slacks would be. One-piece swimsuits may be more acceptable than bikinis. If you are visiting religious sites, take a scarf to cover your head and shoulders.

Coordinate your clothing around a two-color scheme. Add a third or fourth color for accents. If all your items are interchangeable, you can create a wide variety of outfits. Separates will add flexibility. Choose loose, comfortable clothing that will accommodate a security wallet.

If you are handwashing, leave your jeans at home. They are hard to wash by hand and dry very slowly.

All items of clothing should function as part of a layering system. Instead of a few bulky items, pack several thin layers, including insulating underwear, short- and long-sleeved shirts, a sweater, and outergear.

Use accessories to add variety. Colorful belts, hair decorations, hose, and socks do not weigh much. Unless you are traveling where none will be available, take only what makeup and toiletries you need. Use sample sizes or decant products into small plastic bottles. Remember that you have only two clothing colors so you do not need much makeup. If you will be gone a long time, have mom or dad ship you some of your favorite shampoo midway through the trip.

The following wardrobe list is based on the one recommended by the Council on International Educational Exchange (CIEE) in its excellent and highly recommended book *Going Places: The High School Student's Guide to Study, Travel, and Adventure Abroad* (St. Martin's Press 1993). Also refer to the Basic Adventure Wardrobe lists in chapter 7. This wardrobe will fit into a convertible pack and suffice for short or long spring and summer trips. Remember, the less you pack, the more room you have for things you buy!

▼ Travel Wardrobe for Teens

For short trips, pack the minimum number of items recommended. Adjust the mixture of slacks, skirts, and shorts depending on your personal style, the cultural customs of your destination, and your planned activities. Choose light-and medium-weights in easy-care fabrics. Pack a sweater in an accessible place.

Clothes

In your main bag, pack:

Layer 1 – Underlayer

- ▼ 2 T-shirts to go with skirts as well as pants (for boys, polo-type are more versatile)
- ▼ 1 extra-large T-shirt (beach cover-up, nightshirt)
- ▼ 1 pair of leggings or tights to sleep in or for extra warmth

- ▼ 4-7 pairs of underpants
- ▼ 7 pairs of socks
- ▼ 4-5 pairs of hose or tights, if needed (more if you wear an odd size)
- ▼ 2 or 3 bras
- ▼ 1 bathing suit

Layer 2 – Clothing

- ▼ 2 pairs of long pants
- ▼ 1 or 2 skirts
- ▼ 1 short-sleeved blouse or shirt
- ▼ 1 or 2 long-sleeved shirts (1 light for sun protection, 1 heavier)
- ▼ 1 pair of shorts (knee-length)
- ▼ 1 or 2 sweaters or jackets (1 nice, *thin* warm sweater, and 1 sweat-shirt or a casual jacket)
- ▼ 1 dressy outfit in packable fabric, if needed
- ▼ Sport clothing as needed

Layer 3 – Outerwear

- ▼ 1 rainjacket with hood
- ▼ 1 travel umbrella if needed

Layer 4 – Extremities

- ▼ 1 pair of sneakers or walking shoes
- ▼ 1 pair of sandals or thongs
- ▼ 1 pair of dress shoes
- ▼ 1 or 2 belts
- ▼ 1 small, packable purse
- ▼ Bandannas, scarves
- ▼ Cap or packable sun hat
- ▼ Tie, hair accessories, jewelry (not valuable)

Gear for Teens

Also in your main bag, pack the following, not all of which you may need (see chapter 3 for details):

▼ Toiletry kit (with small and sample-sized containers)

▼ Small dual-voltage travel steamer, iron, or hairdryer with appropriate adapter plugs (try to avoid this sort of equipment)

▼ Towel (a Packtowl or half a thin terry towel and a baby washcloth)

▼ Some resealable plastic bags (sandwich and gallon size)

▼ Travel alarm clock

▼ Flashlight and extra batteries

▼ First-aid kit

▼ Sewing kit

▼ Laundry kit

▼ Eating utensils (cup, spoon, fork, plastic plate)

▼ Pictures of your family and home to show new friends

▼ Guidebooks and maps, or photocopied pages in manila envelopes

▼ Fold-up, expandable, nylon totebag

▼ Inflatable pillow and ear plugs for noisy hotels

▼ Small gifts for your hosts

In your daypack or totebag pack:

▼ Eyeglasses and sunglasses

▼ Sunscreen, lip balm

▼ Cosmetic kit (keep it small!)

▼ Water bottle/snack

▼ Pocket knife

▼ Journal or diary, pens, postcards, stationery

▼ Small camera and film

▼ Personal tape player, tapes, headphones

▼ Book, games, cards

▼ Current map, guidebook, brochures

▼ Security for Teens

Some teens think of a money belt as an unnecessary hassle that will spoil their outfits. They also feel immune from theft of important items such as a passport, their traveler's checks, cash, credit cards, phone card, airline tickets, student ID, and so on.

Chances are, nothing will happen. But don't tempt people who are in the business of stealing from unsuspecting travelers. You don't need to be paranoid; just be smart and take responsibility for your personal and material safety. Keep your valuables in a money pouch and wear it *at all times* when you are traveling around, sleeping on the train, or staying in a hostel. Do not leave anything valuable in your luggage or daypack. Wear the pouch hidden *under your clothing*, not hanging around your neck outside your shirt—this is an open invitation to thieves. (I don't even like the neck strap to show under my shirt.)

Luckily, hassle-free security wallets are comfortable and their contents accessible. The best choice is Eagle Creek's Undercover Security Wallet. This vertical pouch has an adjustable strap that you can wear in a variety of ways. The best way to wear it is around your waist, tucked down inside your slacks, skirt, or shorts like a hanging pocket. It is easy to pull in and out, and you don't have to wear a belt. If you are wearing tight pants or skirt (clothes are more comfortable when they are loose-fitting, by the way), the wallet can also be worn around the neck under your shirt (do not let the neck straps show). Or you can shorten the cord and wear the pouch underneath your arm like a holster, or lengthen it and wear it diagonally across your chest, with the pouch tucked into your pants or skirt.

The pouch has three pockets: one long, zippered compartment for traveler's checks, tickets, documents, cash, and so on; an open pocket for your passport and passes; and a third, small zippered pocket on the flap for credit cards and a bit of cash or change. I really like this small pocket: when the pouch is tucked in, you can lift out the flap to have quick access to tip money without having to pull out the whole wallet. For more on security, see the following chapter.

If you develop the skills of packing right and protecting yourself now, you will be prepared to become a real *traveler*, not just a tourist— mobile enough to wander the world, meet wonderful people, and see wonderful places.

10

Security

As a carry-on traveler, you avoid the risk of lost and pilfered luggage. Here are some other precautions you can take to protect yourself and your belongings. For a complete discussion of security and contingency planning, read *The Safe Travel Book* by Peter Savage (Macmillan, 1993). Many of the tips mentioned below come from his book.

▼ Protecting Travel Documents and Valuables

Wear a security wallet *at all times*, whether you are awake or asleep, and hide any visible straps. The best model is the adjustable World Class Passport Carrier by Coconuts, which has a steel cable running through the straps so that it cannot be cut off. Many other types are available. See pp. 36–39 for a full discussion.

Always carry your passport, cash, half of your traveler's checks, your credit cards, address and phone list, and copies of prescriptions in that security wallet. Do not be tempted to pack them anywhere else. To split your risk, carry the remaining half of your traveler's checks in your luggage. Pack your traveler's check record separately from your checks. Keep only a small amount of cash in your wallet or a sturdy nylon pouch you use as a wallet. See pp. 35–36 for a list of "valuables."

Give a home contact copies of all your documents, including the first page of your passport, credit card account numbers, redemption center phone numbers, and itinerary. This person can cancel your credit cards if they are lost or stolen, and send you copies overnight of anything you need quickly.

When making long-distance calls, hide the keypad or use an automatic phone dialer or swipe-through credit card to protect against theft of your account number.

You may store valuables in the hotel safe deposit box if you feel that the hotel security is untrustworthy. Make sure the safe's contents are covered by the hotel's insurance policy. Get a signed, itemized receipt for the items stored.

If you must store valuables in your room, hide them. You can buy hide-a-safes of various sorts, or make a safe by cutting the inner pages out of a paperback book. But the best strategy of all is to travel without valuables.

At the beach, put your valuables in a Seal Pack or other water-tight security wallet (see p. 39) that you can wear while swimming.

As much as possible, use traveler's checks and credit cards instead of cash.

For incidental expenses, carry only a little cash in local currency or small U.S. bills in your daybag, purse, front pocket, fanny pack, or wallet in a front pocket or an inside jacket pocket. *Everything* else should be in your security wallet at all times.

Do not put valuables in a purse and, if someone tugs at your purse, let it go.

Do not wear expensive-looking jewelry and watches. They attract attention.

Include the following phone numbers on your address list, carried in your security wallet:

▼ Your contact person at home who has copies of all documents

▼ The U.S. embassy and the 24-hour telephone number of the U.S. mission. These numbers are available from the State Department in Washington, D.C., (202) 647-4000.

▼ Numbers for reporting lost or stolen credit cards and traveler's check centers (including any after-hours number)

▼ Your travel agent's 24-hour number, if any

▼ Your emergency medical insurance company's 24-hour assistance number or the number of an English-speaking doctor (see IAMAT under Resources)

- ▼ Your automobile insurance company's emergency assistance number

- ▼ Your long-distance calling-card assistance number as well as any additional country codes you may need. When using the telephone, memorize your card code and shield your fingers when inputting your card number (a common scam is for thieves at the airport to steal your card number by watching you punch your number in), or use phones that allow you to slide the card through.

- ▼ Your physician and lawyer

Leave important items that you are unlikely to need while traveling, such as social security and local credit cards, at home.

▼ Luggage

Do not use expensive-looking luggage. It attracts attention. Label each piece of luggage inside and out with your name and *business* address or your next destination. Be sure your luggage is locked. If you check luggage through, watch to make sure it is tagged and routed properly. Attach a luggage strap, colored yarn, or tape to help you identify your bag when you retrieve it. Many bags look alike these days.

At the airport, thieves steal bags off the X-ray machine's conveyor belt while the owner is walking through the metal detector. Make sure that you can go through the detector quickly by putting all metal items, such as large belt buckles, keys, and anything else that might set off the metal detector, inside your carry-on *in advance*. Then, after putting your luggage on the conveyor, do not take your eyes off it. If you are traveling with a companion, take turns going through the detector and watching your luggage.

While waiting, keep your luggage between your ankles. Consider using a retractable cable lock (made by Eagle Creek) to fasten luggage to a bench or fence if you will be waiting long.

Keep any valuables, such as a camera, computer, jewelry, and so on, locked in your daypack or totebag. Most airlines exclude these from liability coverage in checked luggage.

If you want to take a short day trip, check your luggage and equipment at the train station.

In many places, daypacks and purses are commonly slashed and items are stolen without you even noticing. To prevent losing your belongings, you can line the sides and bottoms of your bag or fanny pack with gutter screen to be found at the hardware store.

▼ Medicine

Carry half your medicine with you in your daypack, the other half in your main bag. Carry prescription copies in your security wallet.

▼ Personal Security

IN YOUR HOTEL

- ▼ Maintain heightened awareness at all times; this is your best protection.
- ▼ Be alert when checking in and out of a hotel; do not flash your cash around.
- ▼ Learn the location of hotel exits.
- ▼ Book a room near a busy area or an elevator.
- ▼ Make sure your room has a peephole and double dead bolt locks. You can pack a portable lock (see Resources), such as Portabolt.
- ▼ Call the front desk to verify unexpected deliveries.
- ▼ Small hotels are generally safer than large facilities. Strangers are instantly noticed.
- ▼ Small intruder alarms and smoke alarms are available. Consider these.
- ▼ If brown-outs will be a possibility, carry neon-like lightsticks to use as night lights. They are available at camping-supply stores.

AROUND TOWN

- ▼ Do not look vulnerable or lost. Walk with a purpose and stay alert to what's happening around you.

- ▼ Ask the hotel about the safety of a neighborhood and about areas to be avoided. Ask whether it is safe to walk alone.
- ▼ Ask the concierge for directions and costs before taking a cab.
- ▼ Conventioneers: If you are attending a convention, obtain advance information about the city (maps and guides will be your best source) and, when there, remove your name tag when you are out of the convention area.

IN YOUR RENTAL CAR

- ▼ Have keys in hand when you approach the car. Look in, around, and under the car before getting in.
- ▼ Plan your route before you leave. Tourists stopped at a traffic light and looking at a map are targets for theft and carjackings.
- ▼ Keep your car in gear when stopped at a light.
- ▼ Ask directions from officials.

Remember—most trips are uneventful. Just exercise the same precautions that you do at home, and you are bound to have a safe and enjoyable trip.

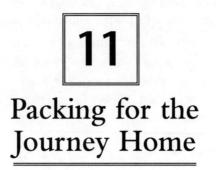

Packing for the Journey Home

By the end of your trip, your clothes are dirty, you're tired, and you just don't care anymore. Am I right? But congratulations, you did it!!

Here are some packing tips for going home:

▼ Check Your List

As you pack, use your packing list to to make sure you didn't forget anything. Keep your list with you. You can review it on the plane coming home, noting things you didn't need and items you wished you had packed. You will also need it for insurance claim purposes should your check-through luggage get lost.

▼ Laundry

Dirty laundry—when your soiled garments are voluminous, your clean bundle is spare. Make a bundle of your clean duds if you're not wearing them, then lay your dirty laundry on top (you can put it in a stuff sack or plastic bag), or place laundry in a separate compartment. Or, put it in your Last Minute Bag and carry it to the laundromat or all the way home.

▼ Pack It In, Pack It Out

Pack the bundle going home the same way you did to leave. Believe it or not, the Bundle Method allows more clothes in the bag than if you folded and stacked them. I packed for my editor for a European business trip (he's 6-foot-something, and had suits), and he couldn't believe that I fit everything into a carry-on. When he got back he said he tried to just stuff it all back in and got nowhere fast! Luckily he remembered the Bundle Method, and he was able to come home without buying another suitcase. Another reason for stowing a foldup nylon bag, just in case.

Packing Shortcut: If you are concerned that the U.S. Customs will inspect the contents of your suitcase, let them! To decrease the time it takes to repack at customs, use the Quick Fix Method before coming home:

1. Lay all your garments in the bag, stacking the collars in one direction.

2. Drape the sleeves out.

3. Drape the bottoms out.

4. Put in your core pouch.

5. To close the bundle, bring all the left sleeves in, then all the right sleeves, then the hems.

Voila! There is your bundle. It is easy to unfurl and close up again if prompted by customs. Remember, don't tempt customs. Have all your paperwork and declarable items ready and waiting to be inspected. By the way, don't forget that by the end of your trip, you will already be a pro using the Bundle Method!

▼ Dealing with Accumulation

What do you do with all of your guidebook pages, maps, tourist brochures, souvenier admissions tickets, and other sundry items you gather along the way? What about purchases? What about film? How do you avoid dragging it all with you?

BUY COMPACT SOUVENIRS

Buy small, compact things instead of big, heavy ones. Items like scarves, jewelry, T-shirts, and fabric are suitable choices. Or, make collections of fun, cheap, easily found items such as postcards, patches, paper money etc. You can pack flat items such as small prints in manila folders and store in flat pockets or underneath your bundle on the divider. Avoid breakables. However, you can pack small breakables in the middle of your bundle, and they will be well cushioned. Or, wrap in a Packtowl or bubble wrap and keep your daypack.

Pack a foldup nylon suitcase, such as the Last Minute Bag, to carry home souvenirs.

Accept the fact that you are going to shop and bring (or buy) a big suitcase, and be prepared to pay the price!

MAIL PACKAGES HOME

Shipping merchandise is the best thing you can do for large and bulky items, even if it is costly. Make shipping a part of your trip budget. This can be a complicated procedure, depending on the country. Only ship from reliable merchants. Otherwise, ship it yourself from a post office. Try to plan your mailing points in advance. Find out as much as you can from other travelers and guidebook information. You may have to devote a lot of time to going to the post office, finding out the rules, going out to buy paper, string, tape, etc. Always carry a permanent marker with you for labeling packages. Put the destination inside the package as well as on the outside. Declare what is inside (be circumspect here). Always watch the complete transaction, then hope for the best. Notify the recipient by separate letter that the package is arriving, and list what is in it so they can check if something is missing.

Paper-based items such as brochures, used maps, guidebooks and photocopied guidebook pages, book admissions tickets, and so on can be packed in 10 × 13-inch manila envelopes labeled with their subject country. When you are done with them, mail them home to yourself.

Carry film home in clear Ziploc bags, or have it developed and mail the prints home. You can also buy prepaid Kodak mailing envelopes from your local dealer before you go, though this can be risky from some countries. Address them to your home or business.

Customs Note: You are allow to mail home goods worth up to $200 of your $400 exemption, provided they are labeled for your personal use and you do not exceed one addressee per day. Used clothing that you brought with you can be shipped home; if it has not been altered, it is exempt. Label the box "American Goods Returned." Bona fide gifts of not more than $50 in fair retail value can be received by friends and relatives in the United States free of duty and tax, if the same person does not receive more than $50 in gift shipments in one day. Perfumes valued at more than $5 retail, tobacco products, and alcoholic beverages are excluded from the gift provision. Gifts for more than one person may be consolidated in the same package provided they are indivdually wrapped and labed with the name of the recipient. Mark the outer wrapping of each package "unsolicited gift" and indicate the nature of gift, and its fair retail value. Mark the box "consolidated gifts" with the names of the recipients listed and the value of each gift. This will facilitate customs clearance of your package.

VAT EXEMPTIONS

When you purchase goods in foreign countries, a 15–20% Value Added Tax (VAT) is paid at point of purchase for many items. Ask for a special VAT exempt invoice when you pay for an item. Keep these VAT receipts with your important documents. Upon leaving the foreign country, you can submit these receipts to the customs agent and the sales tax will be reimbursed to you via mail. Or a voucher may be given to you that you can redeem at a bank in the airport before you leave. Some quick research in a guidebook or a question to your travel agent will help you know what to expect.

CUSTOM GUIDELINES

1. All travelers are allowed a $400 exemption based on the fair retail value of each item in the country where acquired if:

- ▼ the items are for personal or household use;
- ▼ if you bring the items with you at the time of return to the United States and they are properly declared at customs (articles purchased and left for alterations or other reasons cannot be applied to your $400 exemption when shipped to follow at a later date—duty is assessed when received);
- ▼ if you've been gone at least 48 hours (does not apply for Mexico and the U.S. Virgin Islands);
- ▼ or if you have not used this $400 exemption or any part of it within the preceding 30-day period.

A joint declaration for a family returning as a unit can be made with an exemption of $400 for each person regardless of age. Family members making joint declations may combine their personal exemptions, even if the articles acquired by one member of the family exceeds the personal exemption allowed.

Cigarettes, cigars, and liquor have separate requirements. Travelers returning from insular U.S. possessions have different rules. For complete information, contact the U.S. Customs Service. They offer a pamphlet that has complete details, and a website is under construction.

2. Returning U.S. residents and nonresidents must declare:

▼ Articles that you purchased

▼ Gifts presented to you while abroad, such as wedding or birthday gifts

▼ Articles purchased in duty-free shops

▼ Repairs or alternations made to any articles taken abroad and returned, whether or not repairs or alterations were free of charge

▼ Items you have been requested to bring home for another person

▼ Any articles you intend to sell or use in your business

3. *U.S. Customs warns that if you understate the value of an article you declare, or if you otherwise misrepresent an article in your declaration, you may have to pay a penalty in addition to payment of duty. Under certain circumstances, the article could be seized and forfeited if the penalty is not paid.*

4. On the way home, keep your purchases together and your receipts with you in a plastic bag or manila envelope. Have them readily available so that you can fill out the declaration forms on the plane, and so customs can examine them easily. In most cases, the inspection will be perfunctory. Fill out only the identification portion of the Declaration form on the plane. Then you can declare orally your purchases if they fall within the $400 exemption. If you know you have more than this, fill out the entire form with a complete list of merchandise.

DAMAGED LUGGAGE

If you decided to check your luggage through, and it arrives damaged, here is what to do:

1. Check all baggage for damage before leaving the airport. Once you're out the door, it's often too late. Typically, retailers and manufactureres do not cover air carrier damage.

2. Find out the airline's damage liability for baggage. Each allows a certain dollar amount loss per passenger.

3. Damage liability rarely covers loss of valuables, jewelry, cameras, computers and the like.

4. In case of luggage loss, your packing list will come in very handy when you fill out your claim form.

A1

The Top Ten Packing Tips

1. Resolve that you want to travel light.

2. Buy the right luggage. Limit yourself to one main (preferably carry-on size) bag and one smaller tote.

3. Make a packing list after finding out about weather, events, activities, and laundry facilities. When in doubt, leave it out!

4. Choose a color scheme and stick to it.

5 When selecting clothes, pack thin layers for changing temperatures. Know the attributes of various fabrics. Choose simply styled coordinates in maintainable fabrics.

6. For gear, make small kits. Pack toiletries, medical kit, laundry and office supplies in pouches. Use small plastic bottles and sample sizes.

7. Using a checklist, pack all money and valuable documents in a security wallet . Wear it on your body underneath your clothing, even for short trips.

8. Don't forget your photo ID or passport—you can omit almost anything else, but you can't even board the plane without these!

9. Mail home souvenirs, purchases, etc. as you travel so they don't weigh you down.

10. To cut down the next time: Immediately following your trip, review your packing list. Cross out what you didn't need and write down what you wish you had brought. Save this list for the next trip—it will be like gold when it's time to pack again!

Resources

It is amazing how many resources are now available for the traveler. Many luggage, gear, and clothing manufacturers offer catalogs with detailed descriptions of their wares both in paper and on the Internet. You can easily surf the Web to peruse the goods and be referred to a retailer where you can actually go and see the merchandise. Or, you can call and request a product catalog or find out where to go locally to shop. Some companies also take orders directly from consumers.

Besides traditional luggage stores and mail order catalogs, make sure to locate the specialty travel store in your area. These eclectic shops conveniently offer a broad selection of travel books, maps, luggage, travel gear, and sometimes travel clothing. The staff is always knowledgeable and the merchandise is hand-selected by owner and staff.

Luggage and Travel Gear

Easy Going Travel Shop and Bookstore
www.easygoing.com (online catalog sales)
1385 Shattuck Ave., Berkeley, CA 94709 (510)843-3533
1617 Locust St., Walnut Creek, CA 94569 (510) 947-6660
(800) 675-5500 mail orders
e-mail: easygoing@aol.com

Easy Going is close to my heart, because I helped open it in 1979 and worked in it during much of the 1980's. It is a tremendous resource to travelers, and the staff is very knowledgeable and can help you get the things you need.

Many of the items mentioned in this book (and more) are available at both locations of the Easy Going Travel Shop and Bookstore. They sell carry-on and checkable luggage (Easy Going Special Edition

3-Compartment Carry-on Bag; Camp 7 and MEI travel packs; Eagle Creek Cargo Switchback; Travelpro and Atlantic wheelaboards; and Tenba computer bags); organizing aids (including the recommended core pouches such as Carry-Rite Mini-Organizers and Judy Gilford's Deluxe Core Pouch); Stuffed SHIRT Shirt-Frames and Tie-Frames; zippered nylon organizer pouches; "Last Minute" expandable nylon foldup totebags; security wallets (including the World Class Passport Carrier, Undercover Security Wallet, and others); Flexo-line; Packtowls; luggage locks; Remin luggage carts; ultra compact binoculars; dual-voltage travel appliances; standard and heavy duty converters, transformers, and adapters; phone jack adapters; travel soap and spot removers; No-Jet Lag, Earplanes, and Sea Bands; PUR and PurLife water purification devices; and portable raingear. They also have a huge selection of travel books and maps. They have a secured website catalog, and they welcome phone inquiries and mail orders.

LUGGAGE MANUFACTURERS

The following are manufacturers of high-quality, soft-sided luggage and travel packs. Ask for a catalog or the location of a dealer near you.

Luggage and Leather Goods Manufacturers of America (LLGMA)
www.LLGMA.com
350 5th Ave., Suite 2624
New York, NY 10118
(800) 862-4224
e-mail: llgma@llgma.com

This is the luggage industry's official trade organization. Their handy website has a lot of information regarding carry-on regulations of specific airlines, plus a referral service for your local luggage retailer and luggage repair shop.

Andiamo Luggage
www.luggage@Andiamoinc.com
(714) 751-8711

Atlantic Luggage Company
www.atlanticluggage.com
(888) 8-ATLANTIC

Boyt Luggage
(515) 648-6601

Briggs & Reilly
www.briggs-riley.com
(888) HMB-BAGS

Camp 7
(800) 224-2300
www.camp7.com
Travel packs and wheeled travel packs

Delsey Luggage
(800) 558-3344

Eddie Bauer
www.ebauer.com
(800) 789-1386

Eagle Creek Travel Gear
www.eaglecreek.com
(619) 471-2536
Travel Packs as well as standard luggage, travel gear

Hartmann Luggage Co.
www.hartmann.com
(800) 331-0613
Classic designs in leather and nylon

JanSport
www.jansport.com
(800) 5-JANSPORT
Manufacturer of travel packs

Samsonite
www.samsonite.com
(800) 262-8282, ext. 500
This group includes American Tourister and Lark luggage.

Tutto Luggage
www.tutto.com
(800) 949-1288
4-wheeled luggage with pullbars; children's luggage

Travelpro
www.TravelproUSA.com
(561) 998-2824
The originator of wheeled luggage, including the CrewPlus Series (handy plastic divider available separately as a part number)

Specialty Travel Gear

AAA Members Marketplace
www.aaa.com
(800) 327-3190
Peruse the American Automobile Association's online catalog, which features handy stuff for the car. Discount to members. Orders are by phone only.

Campmor
www.campmor.com
(800) 226-7667
Their online and print catalogs offer a wide range of equipment for the traveler and outdoor enthusiast.

Magellan's Catalogue
www.magellans.com
(800) 962-4943
Their well-known online and print catalogs are stocked with lots of travel gear, including mobile computing equipment.

Rand McNally
www.randmcnally.com
(800) 333-0136
Rand McNally offers a wide selection of maps, books and travel gear online and in their many retail locations around the United States.

Solutions
(800) 342-9988
Some neat stuff, including a traveler's emergency dental kit, a personal security flashlight/clock/intruder alarm, and a $5^1/_2$-oz. silk sleep sheet "Dream Sack."

Walkabout Travel Gear
www.walkabouttravelgear.com
(800) 852-7085
Lots of great travel items and luggage in this catalog and on-line catalog.

MOBILE COMPUTING GEAR

TeleAdapt Ltd.
www.teleadapt.com
The Technology Park
Colindeep Lane
London NW9 6TA
UK
Tel +44(0)181 233 3000
Fax +44(0)181 233 3132
Amazing British website and catalog featuring everything you need for mobile computing, plus a help desk to assist you in solving specific connectivity problems anywhere in the world.

COMPUTER AND CAMERA BAGS

Most of the previous luggage manufacturers also make briefcase/computer-type bags. The following are specialists in the field and offer very high-quality, innovative designs.

Lowepro USA
www.lowepro.com
(707) 575-4363

Tenba
www.tenba.com
(212) 966-1013

Tamrac
www.bhphotovideo.com
(800) 606-6969

Photoflex
www.photoflex.com
(800) 486-2674

Travel Clothing

The following catalogs and retailers offer high-quality clothing appropriate for travel. Where noted, other gear and children's clothing are available, too.

Eddie Bauer
www.ebauer.com
(800) 426-6253

Catalog and multiple retail locations. Nice selection of high-quality clothing. Silk underwear is also available seasonally.

Early Winters
(800) 458-4438

This catalog offers a wide array of performance travel clothing and activewear from underwear to casual separates to fleece. A great catalog.

Jaeger International
(800) 7-JAEGER (Mon-Fri 9-5 EST) for locations

This high-end designer retailer is found in major shopping centers around the country. A catalog is also available. Jaeger makes classic daywear separates in incredible British fabrics that are packable, versatile, and beautiful. Even their 100% polyester is amazing. A few investments here will last years and never look out of date. Simple, classic, elegant styling.

L. L. Bean
www.llbean.com
(800) 221-4221

All types of high-quality casual separates and outerwear. Comfort shoes, outdoor gear, and luggage are also included. Silk and polyester thermal underwear seasonally.

Land's End Direct Merchants
www.landsend.com
(800) 356-4444

Wide selection of high-quality, simply styled, durable, casual separates and comfortable shoes. Travelworthy cotton/polyester business shirts and great kits. Silk and polyester knit long underwear seasonally. Lots for kids, too. Also their own line of soft luggage.

Norm Thompson "Departures" Catalog
www.normthompson.com
(800) 547-1160

This Portland, Oregon company's motto, "Escape from the Ordinary," describes their merchandise perfectly. Norm Thompson has an unusual selection of versatile, easy care, classic styles for men and women, including the multi-pocketed Frequent Flyer Travel Jacket. Also features comfortable shoes. They also have three retail stores in Portland.

Patagonia and Patagonia Kids
www.patagonia.com
(800) 638-6464

This catalog features high performance, functional, and attractive clothing for specific climates and activities. Besides great clothing, especially interesting is their "A/C" (air-conditioned) clothing for tropical weather, modest length Baggies shorts, Synchilla fleece clothing, and Capilene polyester knit thermal underwear. Patagonia clothing is also sold through retail dealerships. They sell a fascinating fleece jacket made from recycled soda bottles. This year, they have announced that all their cotton products are from organically grown cotton. Patagonia also features their own luggage line.

The Primary Layer
(800) 282-8206

Nice selection of all types of easy-care underwear including nylon boxer shorts and briefs for men and women, nightwear, socks, etc. They also carry a half slip with hidden pockets for hiding passport and money.

REI – Recreational Equipment Inc.
www.rei.com
(800) 426-4840
TDD: (800) 443-1988

Catalog and multiple retail locations. This excellent retailer offers all kinds of high-performance outdoor equipment, children's packs and carriers, travel packs, clothing, long underwear, shoes, small eating utensils, and other gear. Check out the convertible slacks—long pants that zip off at the knee to become walking shorts.

Royal Robbins
www.royalrobbins.com
(800) 344-7277

Rugged, comfortable cotton "hiking pants," shorts, travel skirts, and shirts. They've expanded their line to include technical fabrics and the "Go Everywhere" line of adventure travel clothing.

Tilley Endurables
www.tilley.com
(800) 338-2797

Catalog and store in Buffalo, NY. This Canadian company offers a variety of "travel and adventure clothing," much of it made of their special "Adventure Cloth"—a cotton/polyester blend that promises easy care and comfort. Coordinated separates allow easy selection of mix and match items, and attractive silk-like microfiber clothing is suitable as packable formalwear. Hats, pants, and shorts are available in a huge selection of sizes for the small, large, and tall person. The famous Tilley Hat comes with a four-page owner's manual and is guaranteed never to wear out.

TravelSmith Outfitting Guide and Catalog
www.travelsmith.com
(800) 950-1600

Unique in its variety and depth of travel clothing, this company offers carefully coordinated wardrobes for different types of trips and climates. Particular attention is paid to layering function, activity, or climate. Technical "adventure" clothing is mixed with a nice offering of casual separates. Each item is described in terms of its layering function, weight, and packability.

The Walk Shop
2120 Vine St.
Berkeley, CA 94709
(510) 849-3628

If you are in the San Francisco Bay Area, check out this excellent selection of comfortable shoes. A very knowledgeable staff can help you make the right selection.

Weekenders Casuals
Chicago, IL
(847) 465-1666 for referral of salesperson in your area

This high-quality, versatile line of highly packable and easily maintained cotton/polyester knit separates is sold by individual consultants nationally. They have a basic "classic" line of nine coordinated pieces (in black, navy, white, and red) available year-round, and a fall/winter and spring/summer line that changes annually based on current designer fashions. Very good for cruises, as well as daywear.

Westwind
725 Santa Cruz Ave., Menlo Park, CA 94025, (415) 329-8876
300 West Portal Ave., San Francisco, CA 94127, (415) 664-2671

This retail women's shop features lightweight, packable, coordinated casual separates arranged by neutral color scheme and group. Colorful accessories, belts, and scarves complete the outfits. Unfortunately, no catalog.

Wintersilks
www.wintersilks.com
(800) 648-7455

Huge year-round selection of silk undergarments, thermal underwear, and clothing for men and women. Nice layering pieces.

Technical and Sun-Protective Clothing

"Sun-protective," "quick-drying," "wrinkle-resistant," "stain-resistant," "abrasion resistant," "comfortable"—these are the attributes of the new genre of travel clothing that has hit the marketplace in the last 10 years. This technical clothing was born in 1986 when Tarponwear, who wanted to design comfortable, cool, and sun-protective clothing for

Florida flats fishermen, combined Dupont-invented Supplex nylon with a vented shirt design to foster air circulation. Supplex is a highly durable fabric that has a soft hand and feels like cotton. It is also so tightly woven that it protects from the UVA and UVB rays of the sun. (They test this in labs, and currently treat fabrics for higher levels of protection.) Who could ask for a better fabric for warm and tropical weather? Dupont also invented Coolmax, a knit fabric which wicks moisture away from the skin 17 times faster than cotton! It is perfect for T-shirts, underwear, and the like. Now there are many blends and styles of travel clothing, but they all achieve the same thing—a packable, comfortable, washable, fast-drying, durable, and attractive travel and active-lifestyle garment. Other technical fabrics include polarfleece, microfiber, and various waterproof, breathable fabrics for rain and wind resistance. See chapter 4 for more information on travel and sunproof clothing.

The following manufacturers make excellent adventure and travel clothing and layering pieces. Check out their websites or call them for a referral of a local retailer who sells their products.

Ex Officio
www.exofficio.com
(206) 283-1471
Ex Officio specializes in technical fabric-based adventure clothing, including the Baja Shirt, the Wayfarer, convertible slacks with zip-off legs, travel skirts, etc. Clothing includes a lot of technical features.

Railriders
(617) 864-5969
Railriders offers three levels of travel clothing, from the highly technical Expedition series, to the more simple, everyday basics line. The middle-range Global Travel Series designs focus on providing pockets and other features important to a traveler "without looking the part of tourist."

Sierra Designs
(800) 635-1461
(Mail order and local dealer referral)
Retail Store
1255 Powell St.

Emeryville, CA 94608

Beautiful pieces for every layer (with function explained on each tag). Favorite basics include the Ray-T-ator "technical" T-shirts, lightweight Sierra fleece cardigan for women, and wonderful, classically styled wool/Spandex black Alpine pants. Also rainwear.

Sun Precautions Inc.

www.solumbra.com

(800) 882-7860

This catalog offers a great selection of casual wear, hats, and accessories, all in 30+ SPF Solumbra fabric.

Tarponwear

www.tarponwear.com

(307) 739-9755

Tarponwear has two collections—their "Original" line designed for flats fishing in 3.1 ounce Supplex fabric, the "Ultra-Dry" lighterweight fabric with a special treatment for quick drying, and the Adventurer series, which includes a ten pocket travel vest. Also Coolmax Polo shirts, T-shirts, and underwear.

Children's Equipment

Land's End

www.landsend.com

(800) 356-4444

Deluxe diaper bag

Tough Traveler

www.toughtraveler.com

(800) 468-6844

1012 State St., Schenectady, NY 12307

Children's travel packs, luggage, daypacks, and child-carriers. Tough Traveler products are also sold through outdoor retailers such as REI.

Gizmo Luggage by Tutto
Tutto Luggage

www.tutto.com

(800) 449-1288

This adorable, brightly-colored, adult-quality line of wheeled luggage and daypacks has reflective tape on all of the models. The 20-inch, 4-wheeled underseat suitcase pulls along easily with a U-shaped pullbar and can be used as a seat or loaded with extras.

Lullaby Lane
(415) 588-7644

This San Francisco Bay Area retailer features a wide selection of items appropriate for traveling with kids, including the 5-point packable safety seatbelt. Also check Toys R Us for many kids' items.

ID Bracelets

Disposable self-closing plastic "I.D. Me" bracelets have a place for name, hotel, etc. written on the underside. Send $1.00 for two bracelets and a long self-addressed, stamped envelope to Practical Parenting, Dept. ID, Deephaven, MN 55391.

Another option is a Medic Alert bracelet. Call Medic Alert Foundation at (800) 344-3226, or check with your drugstore for an order form. Cost is $35.00.

Books

These are books that I have found to be wonderful resources. Available at bookstores and travel stores.

▼ *International Traveler's Weather Guide*, **Tom Loffman (Ten Speed Press, 1996).** A small paperback with complete weather information and descriptions of every destination—a great tool for planning your wardrobe and accessory needs. It is obtainable from Ten Speed Press, P.O. Box 7123, Berkeley, CA 94707.

▼ *Overcoming Jet Lag*, **Dr. Charles F. Ehret and Lynne Waller Scanlon (Berkeley Books, 1983).** All you need to know to minimize the effects of jet lag.

▼ *The Pocket Doctor*, **Stephen Bezruchka, M.D. (Mountaineers, 1992).** This book is a handy, pocket-sized take-along guide that covers first aid and the treatment of a variety of illnesses, bites, infections, and other problems you may encounter on the road.

- ▼ *Backcountry First Aid and Extended Care* (2nd ed.), **Buck Tilton, Director, Wilderness Medicine Institute (ICS Book, Inc., 1994).** Another pocket-sized guide with a focus on the outdoors. Special section on international travel.
- ▼ *The Safe Travel Book*, **Peter Savage (Macmillan, 1993).** With all contingencies considered, this is an amazing resource that helps you plan a truly safe trip.
- ▼ *Staying Healthy in Asia, Africa and Latin America*, **Dirk Schroeder (Moon Publications, 1993).** This comprehensive handbook explains medical and health procedures for those traveling to developing countries.

Medical Assistance

IAMAT (International Association for Medical Assistance to Travelers)
736 Center St.
Lewiston, NY 14092
(716) 754-4883

IAMAT will give you the names of English-speaking physicians and the locations of hospitals around the world, as well as climate, immunization, and sanitation information.

Questions and Answers

Here are answers to the questions that I get asked most frequently during my packing classes:

What is the best fabric for travel?

Natural fibers, such as pure cotton and wool, breathe the best, but synthetics, such as polyester, lend wrinkle- and stain-resistance and dry faster. Wool and wool/blend gabardine are superior for fall, winter, and spring. Cotton and cotton/blend knits are perfect for spring and summer. (See the fabric chart on p. 73 for recommended travel fabrics.)

How many garments can you fit in a suitcase?

Almost every person can pack a basic travel wardrobe (between seven and nine pieces) in a carry-on. How much more you can get in will depend on your size and the length and bulk of your garments. Generally, smaller people will be able to pack between ten and sixteen pieces; larger people possibly no more than the minimum seven or eight. Your jacket is the bulkiest item. If you don't pack that, you will have more room for other clothing.

Does this packing system work for larger shoe and clothing sizes?

The beauty of the Bundle Method (see chapter 5) is that everyone can use it. The number of items of clothing you can fit may, however, be limited by your size. People with larger shoes will need to consolidate as much as possible. If both shoes cannot fit along the bottom edge of the bag, you will need to sacrifice other space. The best strategies are to wear one pair and pack one pair or to take a second bag.

What is the rule of thumb about underwear and socks?

It depends on how much you want to wash. To travel extremely light, take two pairs of each and wash one and wear one. Take eight pairs if you want to wash once a week. I generally take four or five pairs of each. Take an extra pair in cold weather, because things dry more slowly then.

What about galoshes?

Galoshes are great if you are going to very wet weather. They seem to be difficult to find these days, but if you find a lightweight pair, buy it.

How long does it take you to pack?

The hard part of packing is selecting the clothing. Once you have your wardrobe, you will pack clothing in five minutes or less. Replacing accessories takes longer than repacking the clothes.

I tried the Bundle Method and things still got wrinkled. What am I doing wrong?

Two things could have happened. First, the fabrics you chose may not have traveled well. Second, you may not have packed tightly enough. For the Bundle Method to work, the core and inner items must provide sufficient cushioning and the outer layers must be wrapped tightly around the core. If they are loose or underpacked, more wrinkling will occur.

Do you use plastic dry-cleaning bags and tissue paper?

Plastic dry cleaning bags are great. The positive side of using plastic is that it reduces friction and allows fabrics to fall naturally, thereby minimizing creasing. Plastic is useful when wrinkle-free appearance is of the highest priority. It is useful in suitcases, suiters, and garment bags when suits, dresses, and wrinkle-prone blouses and shirts are packed on hangers. You may use it if clothing is folded in half, such as when it is hung in a garment bag or a wheelaboard "suiter," packed on hangers using the Z-fold method, or folded over in a larger suitcase or duffel bag.

However, if I have a full wardrobe or a casual wardrobe I do not use plastic for the Bundle Method because the plastic takes up a lot of room in the bag and promotes the shifting of clothing, thereby making it difficult to pack. In hot weather, plastic traps moisture and promotes wrinkling. Also, if fabrics are appropriately chosen, the need for plastic is minimized, if not eliminated.

I only use tissue paper if I want to cushion a crease. In this case you can stuff sleeves and put some under collars, or other folds.

Do you pack hangers?

I generally pack one small plastic or metal skirt hanger since hotels often don't have them. It goes in my accessory section. I sometimes pack clothing on hangers with plastic dry cleaning bags using the Z-fold method (see p. 114).

If you are going to be in a different place every day, would you still use the Bundle Method?

Yes! Of course, it is a bit different from being able to reach in and pull out one folded garment. The trade-off is you will have less creasing and spend less time ironing. Don't forget—with your efficient travel wardrobe, you will only be working with five to seven packed garments. You will get really quick at folding and unfolding the bundle.

Here are a few tips if you cannot unpack completely:

▼ Pack separates. They are easier to pack and unpack. To remove an inner item you need only unfurl one or two items, reach your hand in, and slip out what is needed.

▼ When you arrive at your hotel, open your suitcase and unfurl the bundle. Let the sleeves and bottoms hang out of the sides of the bag. This will make each item accessible to you and give garments a chance to breathe and rest. Hang up your core pouch. In the morning, simply refold the bundle.

▼ Learn to think ahead about what you will need. Keep what you will want access to out of the bundle and either lay it on top or tuck it in the corners of your bag.

What is the difference between steamers and irons?

Steamers remove wrinkles from light- and medium-weight, absorbent fabrics, such as wool, silk, and synthetic blends. They do not work well on heavier weights of cotton. If you want a pressed, crisp look, an iron will be necessary.

How do you tie on the Flexo-line?

If you have a shower you can loop-knot the clothesline around the bathtub rod and stretch it across to the shower head, looping it over. The line can also be doubled back on itself, if necessary.
PS Dental floss makes a handy clothesline.

Is there a product for a travel laundry kit that would take care of mildew?

The best way to take care of mildew is to wash in the hottest water safe for the fabric. If the stain remains, soak the garment in warm water with a nonchlorine bleach and wash it again. The sun is also a natural bleach: Treat fresh mildew with lemon juice and salt and dry the garment in direct sunlight. Rinse and rewash the garment. Old mildew stains are almost impossible to remove.

How do you carry medicines?

Get your prescription medicine in two, separately labeled, small bottles. Keep half your supply in your daybag and half in your main bag, so that, if you lose one bag, you will still have your medicine. If you need to refrigerate medicine, carry a lightweight insulated bag with an icepack. Refreeze the pack each night at your hotel.

How does one prevent bottles of shampoo and so on from leaking when carried on airplanes?

To prevent leaks, fill your bottles two-thirds full, squeeze out the air, and close them. You can tape the caps for additional protection.

How do you keep lipstick from melting in hot weather?

Try using lip pencil instead of lipstick.

Isn't a security wallet hot to wear?

Unfortunately, there is no way around it—in hot weather anything against your body seems hot. The best way to wear a security wallet in hot weather is as a loop-wallet, so that it is tucked inside your slacks or skirt and rests on your thigh, where it is easily accessible. Both the World Class Passport Carrier by Coconuts and Eagle Creek's Undercover Security Wallet can be worn like this. If you prefer a waist money pouch, choose one with a comfortable absorbent backing, such as Cambrelle or cotton.

Are security wallets waterproof?

All security wallets are water-repellent, so that they will resist perspiration moisture. In very warm weather, the contents can, however, become damp. You can provide extra protection by encasing the contents in a Ziploc bag or the waterproof, resealable cover made by Omniseal. If you want to swim with your valuables, use a Seal Pack or other watertight wallet that is specifically designed to be submersible in water.

How much does a typical carry-on bag weigh when full?

My one bag with two wardrobes and all accessories weighs 25 pounds. This is about the most you would want to pack. If you take two bags, you can divide this weight, which will make the luggage easier to carry.

Does a 45-inch carry-on bag really fit under the seat?

Forty-five-inch bags (up to 22 inches long) go under the seat in most planes. Rigid-frame bags, however, are more difficult to maneuver into place. Commuter or trans-Pacific flights, smaller aircraft, and aisle seats will be exceptions and may accommodate only 20-inch bags. Check the carry-on regulations for your airlines before you buy your luggage.

Aren't luggage carts a hassle?

This depends entirely on your situation. The lack of a luggage cart is a hassle if you have more than one bag. Carts are also versatile. They offer wider wheels and stepsliders for added stability and you can use them with any bag you already own. They do require that you stop and unload and collapse them before boarding the plane, and they must be stored separately. If you need only one carry-on and are planning to buy a bag, then wheeled luggage, such as the Rollaboard by Travelpro, will eliminate the need for an extra piece.

Does the steel cable in the World Class Passport Carrier by Coconuts set off the metal detector at the airport?

No, I've never heard of that happening.

What length of knife is allowed on an airplane?

The blade must be no more than 4 inches long to be allowed on the airplane. This goes for scissors, too. Pack your knife in your carry-on. If it is in your pocket, it may be confiscated until the end of the flight.

What do you do if U.S. Customs wants to inspect your belongings?

Let them! To decrease the time it takes to repack in case customs asks you to undo your bundle, use the Quick-Fix Method before coming home: Lay all your garments in the bag, stacking the collars in one direction. Drape the sleeves out. Drape the bottoms out. Put in your core. To close the bundle, bring all the left sleeves in, then all the right sleeves. Then the bottom. Voila! There is your bundle. It is easy to unfurl and to close up again if you get stopped at customs. Remember, don't tempt customs. Have all your paperwork and declarable items ready and waiting to be inspected.

A4

The Last Minute Packer's Quicklists

▼ Planning in a Nutshell

There's no way around it—packing less means planning more, at least the first few times you travel this way. Start this process as soon as you confirm your travel plans:

Resolve that you want to travel light. This may be the hardest thing to do, but it has a major payoff in the end. Trust me, it's true.

Start a preliminary packing list. The following information will direct it:

1. Find out about the weather, local customs, and conditions—note clothing and gear needed. Think about what types of fabrics will provide the functions you need, and which layer pieces you may need. Consider style as well.

2. Write down your planned activities and events—note clothing and gear needed.

3. Take note of things you absolutely can't do without to make you a happy traveler, even if they seem frivolous—you'll make up for the added load by cutting back somewhere else.

4. Peruse the checklists in this book. See if they remind you of something you need or haven't thought of. Make notes on your list.

5. Call your hotel(s) to confirm amenities, such as hairdryers. Discuss with your travel companion who will carry what (don't duplicate). Eliminate from your list gear you don't need.

6. Decide how you will do your laundry on the road. Hand wash? Dry clean? Determine appropriate fabrics you need.

7. Review your wardrobe for suitable clothing, accessories, and, shoes. Make outfits and note items needed to complete them. Choose a color scheme and stick to it.

8. Refine your packing list. Cut down wherever possible. Be ruthless!

9. Shop at stores, through catalogs, and online. Give yourself as much time as possible. Shop in fall and winter for warm-weather basics, such as thinly knit wool sweaters and tops.

10. Assemble your medical, toiletry, and other kits. Little items take forever to assemble and are easily forgotten at the last minute (see chapter 3). Always keep them at the ready for carefree packing.

11. Practice packing. See what fits and what can be eliminated. Try to carry it a distance. If it's too heavy, eliminate more. (Go back to #1 if you're having trouble here!)

12. After your trip, review your list. Cross out items you didn't need and write down things you wished you had packed. Store this list in your suitcase, security wallet, or on your computer. Next time, you'll use this information to cut down even more.

▼ Last Minute Packer's To Do List

Here's what needs to be done in the few days before you leave:

☐ Check the current weather at destination(s).

☐ Finalize your packing list; do last minute shopping.

☐ Wash clothes.

☐ Pick up dry cleaning

☐ Pick up traveler's checks.

☐ Get foreign cash—at least $50 in each denomination.

☐ Get $1 bills for tips.

☐ Establish PIN numbers for your credit and ATM cards.

☐ Assemble all your travel clothing, including underwear, socks, shoes, accessories.

- [ ] Get out your suitcase or garment bag and daybag.
- [ ] Gather your packing aids—organizer pouches or Ziploc bags, core pouch, shoe covers, plastic dry cleaning bags, hangers, plastic bag for wet or soiled items, etc.
- [ ] Make up your medical, toiletry, and other kits (see below).
- [ ] Pack your valuable documents, tickets and money in your security wallet (don't forget photo ID and/or passport—you can't even get on the plane without these!!)
- [ ] Charge your computer, cell phone, etc.
- [ ] Set cell phone for roaming.
- [ ] Pack your business case, totebag, or daypack. This can be heavy and go underseat.
- [ ] Pack your suitcase. Keep it as light as possible so you can lift it overhead.

▼ Leaving Home Quicklist

- [ ] Choose a home contact who will able to send you anything you need in an emergency. Make a contact book for your home contact with copies of all your documents,itineraries, phone numbers, information, emergency information etc. (see p. 40).
- [ ] Make a binder of information for caregivers if you are leaving your children at home—local emergency numbers; medical, dental, and allergy information; medical authorization; friends' and schools' phone numbers; maps; children's schedule; directions; etc. Arrange for rides to and from activities, if needed. Notify friends that you will be away. Review the children's plan and your itinerary with your children before you leave
- [ ] Stop the newspaper.
- [ ] Stop the mail and all deliveries, or ask a neighbor to collect all deliveries.
- [ ] Pay your bills before you leave or arrange for someone else to do so.
- [ ] Plug in timers to turn on lights and a radio or television.

- [ ] Lock all doors and windows.
- [ ] Don't change phone message on answering machine.
- [ ] Arrange with neighbors for the garbage cans to be put out on the curb and replaced after pickup.
- [ ] Arrange for gardener to keep up the yard.
- [ ] Look like you're home—leave curtains and blinds in normal position, park your car in the driveway or ask a neighbor to park there periodically.
- [ ] Consider taking valuables to a safe deposit box.
- [ ] Engrave your valuables. If something is stolen it has a better chance of being retrieved.

These lists come in handy when you're packing in a hurry.

The Bare Essentials Checklist

- [ ] security wallet (contents pp. 39–40)
- [ ] important documents (contents pp. 40–41)
- [ ] travel alarm clock or watch with alarm
- [ ] toiletry kit
- [ ] medical/first-aid kit
- [ ] clothing care kit
- [ ] travel umbrella, packable raincoat
- [ ] hat/sunscreen/insect repellent
- [ ] water bottle(with purifier, if needed)/snack
- [ ] flashlight or reading light/batteries
- [ ] pocketknife
- [ ] notebook and pen
- [ ] book/portable tape or CD player
- [ ] small camera, film, batteries
- [ ] set of earplugs
- [ ] plastic bag for wet or soiled items
- [ ] foldup, expandable, nylon totebag
- [ ] photographs of your family

▼ Organizing Yourself

The Basic Bags

- ☐ your main bag (21- or 22-inch carry-on, or 24-inch checkable bag, or garment bag)
- ☐ your daybag (daypack, duffel, tote, etc.)
- ☐ last-minute bag (can be your daybag)
- ☐ security wallet
- ☐ day wallet or nylon pouch
- ☐ core pouch(es)—one for each bundle
- ☐ bags for kits—plastic resealable bags, nylon organizer bags, stuff sacks, etc.
- ☐ shoe covers

Main Suitcase Checklist

Try to keep this bag light enough to lift overhead. Pack heavy items in your daybag so you can stow them under the seat.

- ☐ luggage ID inside and out
- ☐ luggage lock
- ☐ manila-envelope documents, with itinerary, trip notes
- ☐ clothing
- ☐ shoes
- ☐ lingerie
- ☐ handbag
- ☐ non-inflight gear, including:
  - ☐ travel clock
  - ☐ clothing care kit
  - ☐ picnic kit
  - ☐ water purifier
  - ☐ extra batteries
  - ☐ small appliances, cell phone charger
  - ☐ half of prescription medicine
  - ☐ small gifts

- ☐ outside pockets, if any:
  - ☐ stowable raincoat
  - ☐ hat
  - ☐ toiletry kit
  - ☐ foldup, expandible, nylon tote
  - ☐ small umbrella

Daybag Checklist

OUTSIDE POCKETS:

- ☐ luggage lock
- ☐ luggage ID inside and out
- ☐ boarding passes, customs documents, receipts, local currency
- ☐ any other documents you need accesible for boarding and leaving the plane or train
- ☐ addresses
- ☐ pen and notebook, or office supply kit
- ☐ emergency items: knife, flashlight, compass, tool kit
- ☐ bandana, handkerchief
- ☐ prescription medicines, cup
- ☐ first-aid kit

MIDDLE OF BAG:

In-flight toiletry kits: moist towelettes, toilet-seat covers, sanitary items, toothbrush and toothpaste, mints or mouthwash, comb, lip balm, moisturizer, headache reliever, antacid, antihistimine, etc.

- ☐ eyecare supplies
- ☐ cosmetics/pocket mirror
- ☐ water bottle, snack
- ☐ family photos (in plastic cover)
- ☐ wallet (for minimal cash, receipts only)
- ☐ coin purse
- ☐ eyeglasses, sunglasses
- ☐ in-flight reading material, work

- [ ] computer and computer equipment
- [ ] cell phone, pager
- [ ] walkman, tapes
- [ ] in-flight accessories:
  - [ ] travel pillow
  - [ ] eyeshades
  - [ ] earplugs
  - [ ] jet lag remedy, melatonin, dramamine, etc.
  - [ ] thick socks or slippers
  - [ ] flashlight
  - [ ] phrasebook, guidebook
  - [ ] map/magnifier/highlighter pen

BOTTOM OF BAG:

- [ ] jewelry
- [ ] sweater or jacket
- [ ] umbrella
- [ ] keys
- [ ] camera and film
- [ ] half of your traveler's checks
- [ ] important documents, vouchers, receipts (see pp. 40–41)
- [ ] small appliances

Security Wallet Checklist

- [ ] photo ID
- [ ] passport
- [ ] credit cards
- [ ] ATM card
- [ ] cash, U.S. and local currency
- [ ] traveler's checks
- [ ] checks
- [ ] long distance calling card
- [ ] tickets
- [ ] driver's license
- [ ] auto club card
- [ ] copies of medical and eyeglass prescriptions

- 3 × 5-inch card with emergency phone numbers and medical allergies
- student ID card
- train pass or voucher
- address list
- visa(s)
- extra passport photos
- other documents (see pp. 40–41).

Toiletry Kit (small sizes only)

These items are often forgotten on the day of travel, so make a duplicate kit that is ready to go at all times.

HOTEL WITH AMENITIES TRIP:

- eyecare supplies
- facial cleanser
- toothbrush/holder or cap
- toothpaste
- dental floss
- antiperspirant
- razor or shaver/blades
- shaving cream
- nail clipper
- travel soap
- comb/folding brush
- pocket mirror

SELF-SUFFICIENT TRIP ADD:

- shampoo
- conditioner
- moisturizer
- hairdryer (dual-voltage with adapter plugs for foreign travel)

Makeup/Beauty

- ☐ foundation
- ☐ eyeshadow
- ☐ blush
- ☐ lip pencil
- ☐ lipstick
- ☐ mascara
- ☐ eye pencil
- ☐ other_____

Health/First Aid Kit

- ☐ sufficient supply of all prescription medications
- ☐ antidiarrhea medication (i.e., Pepto-Bismol tablets)
- ☐ acetaminophen or ibuprofen
- ☐ antacid (i.e., Alka Seltzer tablets)
- ☐ antiseptic pads
- ☐ antibiotic ointment (for cuts and scratches)/cotton swabs
- ☐ anti-itch balm or 1% hydrocortisone cream (for insect bites)
- ☐ adhesive tape, gauze bandages, first-aid strips, etc.
- ☐ motion sickness remedy
- ☐ sunscreen
- ☐ lip balm
- ☐ decongestant or antihistamine
- ☐ insect repellent
- ☐ thermometer (nonmercury)
- ☐ travel dental kit
- ☐ water purification tablets or equipment, if needed

Clothing Care Kit

- ☐ sewing kit
- ☐ multipurpose travel soap

- ☐ stain treatment
- ☐ clothesline/clips
- ☐ inflatable hanger
- ☐ sink stopper
- ☐ shoe shine pads, if needed
- ☐ plastic bag for wet or soiled clothing
- ☐ Packtowl
- ☐ lintbrush
- ☐ steamer, iron, or wrinkle-remover spray

Emergency Kit

For that "just in case" level of protection, carry the following in a small, plastic, resealable bag or a small nylon pouch. Tuck it in your purse, pocket, briefcase, or inside your underwear! You can find individually wrapped, first-aid and nonprescription drugs in pharmacies and well-stocked travel stores.

- ☐ antiseptic pad
- ☐ antibiotic ointment
- ☐ Band-Aids, gauze bandage
- ☐ moist towellettes
- ☐ ibuprofen
- ☐ Pepto-Bismol tablets
- ☐ tiny sewing kit with needle and thread, buttons, safety pins
- ☐ a few tissues
- ☐ folded-up toilet seat cover
- ☐ personal hygiene pad, tampon
- ☐ condom

Picnic Kit

- ☐ spoon
- ☐ pocket knife
- ☐ hot/cold cup

☐ cutting board

☐ dual-voltage beverage heater (with adapter plugs)

☐ Packtowl wipe-up cloth

☐ small plastic plate (optional)

☐ bottle stopper

Emergency Card

In your security wallet, carry a 3 × 5-inch card with the following information. (Also put copies of the card, *minus your credit card number and social security number*, in your companion's luggage and in each piece of your own luggage.)

☐ home contact phone number

☐ credit card number

☐ phone number to report lost credit card

☐ travel agent

☐ doctor

☐ lawyer

☐ social security number

☐ codes (if any)

☐ passport number

☐ drivers license number

(This tip courtesy of Mrs. M. Valois, Sierra Madre, CA)

For Office Supplies see pp. 58–59

For Computer Equipment see p. 59

For Women's Packing List see p. 97

For Men's Packing List see p. 98

For Business Travel see pp. 135–136

A5

Fabrics and Clothing Care

Following is a complete stain removal guide. It is meant for the traveler who would like to be prepared for all kinds of stains, and is especially helpful for families. Of course, professional dry cleaning is recommended for all dry-cleanables. For a great book on stain removal, use Don Aslett's *Stain Buster's Bible* (NAL-Dutton, 1990).

Be aware that all garments and stains are unique. While these are generally recommended techniques, author and publisher claim no liability should garment be ruined.

To be fully prepared for stains, carry in one-ounce bottles or plastic baggies, or buy upon arrival:

▼ one-ounce bottle of white vinegar (for tomato-based stains)

▼ one-ounce bottle of ammonia

▼ plastic resealable bag of enzyme detergent such as Biz

▼ one solid stick soil and stain treatment (laundry pre-wash)

▼ Swiss Care Paste all-purpose stain treatment

▼ one small can Goddard's Nonflammable Dry-Cleaning Solvent

▼ spot remover pads (for wool and silk)

▼ digestant (available from pharmacy) for protein stains

Other items you've already packed that are handy for stain removal—dull side of your pocketknife for scraping off excess material; Packtowl washcloth for sponging, absorbing; salt or talcum powder as absorbent; club soda or water from your water bottle for keeping stains wet until treatment; neutral detergent (Biosuds or multipurpose travel detergent).

▼ Stain Removal Guide

Stain	Remedy
Alcoholic beverages (beer, liquor)	Sponge or soak fresh stains with cold water. Wash. If stain remains, soak for 15 minutes in a solution of lukewarm water, liquid detergent, and a few drops of white vinegar. Rinse and re-wash. Dry-cleanables: Take to dry cleaner immediately.
Baby food	Soak in cold water. While still wet, rub detergent into stain. Wash garment with chlorine bleach and detergent in hottest water safe for fabric. If bleach can't be used, soak garment in warm water and an enzyme-containing pre-wash before washing.
Baby formula, milk, ice cream, cream (not chocolate)	Blot up excess. Apply pre-wash soil and stain remover or soak in enzyme detergent for 30 minutes to 1 hour in warm water. Wash in warm water. Dry-cleanables: Sponge with spot remover pad, then rinse with water and air dry. If stain remains, spot with dry-cleaning solvent.
Blood	*Don't let it dry.* Rinse, sponge, or soak in cold water. Rub detergent into any remaining stains. Rinse. If stain remains apply a few drops 3% hydrogen peroxide on stain for 3-5 minutes. Rinse thoroughly. Wash in cold water. Dry-cleanables: Dilute a few drops of ammonia with cold water, and sponge stain thoroughly. Don't use ammonia on wool or silk.
Chocolate, chocolate ice cream	Washables: Apply a pre-wash soil and stain remover. Wash. If stain remains, apply a liquid detergent or soak in warm water with enzyme pre-soak. Re-wash. Dry-cleanables: Sponge immediately with a dry-cleaning solvent or Swiss Care.
Coffee/tea	Don't let it dry out. Sponge with cool water. Washables: Apply pre-wash soil and stain remover, wash in warm water, air dry. Dry-cleanables: Sponge with spot remover pad and a few drops of vinegar, flush with cool water.

Stain	Remedy
Deodorant/ antiperspirant	Treat with liquid detergent or your regular laundry detergent. Wash in the hottest water that's safe for the fabric. Heavy stains: Make a paste of ammonia and *non-chlorine* bleach, and apply on the wrong side of the stain. Let stand for 30 minutes. Wash in the hottest water the fabric can take.
Fat, grease, or oil	Washables: Use laundry pre-treat or treat with liquid detergent. Follow label directions. Wash in hottest water safe for fabric. Dry-cleanables: Use talcum powder or salt to absorb as much excess as possible. Remove absorbent. Apply dry-cleaning solvent (Goddard's or Swiss Care).
Feces and urine	Washables: Scrape off all excess. Don't rub it in. Treat stain with stain remover or soak in enzyme-containing pre-wash. Wash with detergent and chlorine or all-fabric bleach. If stain remains, rub with a paste of detergent and water. Re-wash.
Fruit and fruit juice, red wine	Washables: DO NOT USE SOAP. Rinse immediately in cool water. Apply water diluted with a few drops of vinegar and rinse. Air dry. If stain remains, apply laundry soil and stain remover, wash with detergent and bleach in warm water. Air dry.
Grass or green vegetables	Washables: Treat stain with a stain remover or soak in enzyme prewash. Wash with detergent and chlorine or all-fabric bleach. If stain is still there, rub with alcohol (dilute with two parts water if colorfastness is a concern or if the fabric is acetate) while flushing with the hottest water the fabric can take. Dry-cleanables: Sponge with alcohol (test for colorfastness). For acetate, dilute alcohol with two parts water. Do not use alcohol on wool. If stain remains, sponge with vinegar, then with water.

Stain	Remedy
Ink, ballpoint	Washables: Apply Magic Wand or spray the stain with an aerosol hair spray, acetone, or rubbing alcohol (do not use acetone on acetate, triacetate, or modacrylics). Sponge stain continuously until all bleeding stops. Air dry. Repeat if necessary. Wash. If stain remains, bleach if it's safe for the fabric. Dry-cleanables: Take in for professional cleaning immediately.
Ink, felt tip (washable)	Washables: Sponge with Goddard's. Apply laundry stick and a few drops of ammonia (don't use ammonia on silk or wool), and launder in warm water. Dry-cleanables: Take in for professional cleaning.
Lipstick	Washables: Apply Goddard's or pre-wash soil and stain remover. Blot with absorbent. Repeat if necessary. Rinse. If stain remains, rub with liquid detergent. Wash. Dry-cleanables: Apply Goddard's, Swiss Care, or other stain remover intended to remove makeup. Be careful not to spread the stain. Sponge any remaining dye stain with spot-remover pads and a few drops of ammonia (don't use ammonia on silk or wool). Rinse in warm water.
Lotions	Washables: Apply laundry pre-treat and wash in hot water. Dry-cleanables: Sponge repeatedly with Goddard's or Swiss Care until stain is gone.
Makeup	Washables: Carefully scrape or brush off excess. Blot with Goddard's, being careful not to spread the stain. If color remains, apply vegetable or mineral oil for 15 minutes, and sponge again with Goddard's. Sponge any remaining dye stain with spot-remover pads and a few drops of ammonia (do not use ammonia on silk or wool). Apply laundry pretreatment product and launder washables in hot water if safe for the fabric. Dry-cleanables: Scrape or blot all excess. Apply dry-cleaning solvent or Swiss Care. Remove as directed. If dye remains, repeat process or use a spot-remover pad. A few drops of ammonia can be applied (except to silk or wool). Sponge-rinse with warm water.

Stain	Remedy
Mildew	Washables: Wash in the hottest water that's safe for the fabric. If stain remains, soak in warm water and non-chlorine bleach for 15-30 minutes. Re-wash. As an alternative to bleach, treat with salt and lemon juice and dry in direct sunlight. Rinse and re-wash. Dry-cleanables: Take in for professional cleaning. Note: Old mildew stains are almost impossible to remove.
Mustard, curry, or turmeric	Treat *immediately*. Scrape off excess mustard with credit card or dull side of a knife blade. Sponge with a non-flammable dry-cleaning agent or a pre-wash soil and stain remover. Rinse. Work liquid detergent and a few drops of vinegar into the stain. Rinse. If the stain remains, apply 3% hydrogen peroxide. Rinse and wash.
Perspiration	You can prevent perspiration stains by wearing garment shields. Washables: Remove stains before ironing. Wash or sponge fresh stains thoroughly with detergent and warm water. If perspiration has changed the color of the fabric, apply ammonia to stain. Rinse. Launder to remove ammonia odor. Dry-cleanables: Sponge with non-flammable dry-cleaning solvent, then with spot-remover pads and a few drops of ammonia (but don't use ammonia on silk or wool). Flush with water.
Protein stains (meat, egg)	Washables: Scrape off excess with dull side of knife or credit card. Soak in cold or warm water with enzyme pre-soak for at least 30 minutes. Treat grease stains with Goddard's or Swiss Care. Wash. Dry-cleanables: Treat with Goddard's or Swiss Care.
Soy sauce	Washables: Sponge with diluted vinegar. Apply laundry pre-treat. Launder in cold water. If stain remains, soak in Biz, launder in cold water. Dry-cleanables: Sponge with spot remover pads. Dilute a few drops of vinegar, rinse with cool water. (No water on non-prewashed silks.)

Stain	Remedy
Tar	Washables: Sponge with dry-cleaning solvent until completely removed. Work from the outside in, so as not to spread the stain. When stain is gone, apply laundry pre-treat and launder in hot water. Dry-cleanables: Apply dry-cleaning solvent. If stain remains, take to a professional cleaner.
Tomato products and sauces	Washables: Sponge with cool water. Apply laundry pre-treat, and rinse. If stain is gone, launder in warm water. If stain remains, sponge with a solution of half vinegar and half water, and rinse again. Reapply laundry pre-treat and wash in warm water. Dry-cleanables: Sponge with cool water and let dry. Sponge with Goddard's or Swiss Care. If stain remains, sponge with solution of half vinegar and half water, then rinse.
Vomit	Washables: Treat with stain remover or soak in enzyme-containing pre-wash. Wash with detergent and bleach safe for fabric. Dry-cleanables: Apply stain removal liquid and a few drops of ammonia (no ammonia on wool or silk). Sponge-rinse with cool water. If stain remains, make a paste of digestant (Biz or unseasoned meat tenderizer), apply and leave on half an hour. (No digestant on silk or wool.) Rinse with warm water and wipe gently from center of stain outward to blend. If stain is still present, use Goddard's, Swiss Care, or bleach with hydrogen peroxide.

Bibliography

Allen, Jeanne. *Showing Your Colors: A Designer's Guide to Coordinating Your Wardrobe* (Chronicle Books, 1986).

Angelucci, Diane Donofrio. "Washday Stain-Removal Chart," *Baby Talk*, August 1993.

Aslett, Don. *Stain Buster's Bible: The Complete Guide to Stain Removal* (NAL-Dutton, 1990).

Axtell, Roger E. *Do's and Taboos Around the World*, 3rd ed. (Wiley, 1993).

Brown, George Albert. *The Airline Passenger's Guerrilla Handbook: Strategies and Tactics for Beating the Air Travel System* (Blakes Publishing Group, 1989).

Butler, Arlene Kay. *Traveling with Children and Enjoying It: A Complete Guide to Family Travel by Car, Plane, and Train* (Globe Pequot, 1991).

"Carry-on Luggage," *Consumer Reports*, October 1987.

Cass, Lee Hogan, and Karen E. Anderson. *Look Like a Winner: Why, When, and Where to Wear What* (Putnam, 1985).

Consumer Report Books editors, with Monte Florman and Marjorie Florman, *How to Clean Practically Anything* (Consumer Report Books, 1992).

Council on International Educational Exchange. *Going Places: The High-School Student's Guide to Study, Travel and Adventure* (St. Martin's Press, 1993).

Evatt, Cris. *How to Pack Your Suitcase . . . and Other Travel Tips* (Fawcett Columbine, 1987).

Feldon, Leah. *Traveling Light: Every Woman's Guide to Getting There in Style* (Putnam, 1985).

"Foiling Baggage Thieves," *Kiplinger's Personal Finance*, November 1995.

Green, Mary and Stanley Gillmar. *How to Be an Importer and Pay For Your World Travel.* (Ten Speed Press).

Harriman, Cynthia W. *Take Your Kids to Europe* (Mason-Grant, 1991).

Hatt, John. *The Tropical Traveller: An Essential Guide to Travel in Hot Climates* (Hippocrene, 1984).

Jeffrey, Nan, with Kevin Jeffrey. *Adventuring with Children: The Family Pack-Along Guide to the Outdoors and the World* (Foghorn Press, 1992).

Koltun, Frances. *Complete Book for the Intelligent Woman Traveler* (Simon and Schuster, 1967).

Lansky, Vicki. *Trouble-Free Travel with Children: Helpful Hints for Parents on the Go* (The Book Peddlers, 1991).

Loffman, Tom. *International Traveler's Weather Guide* (Ten Speed Press, 1996).

Nwanna, Gladson I. *Americans Traveling Abroad: What You Should Know Before You Go.* (World Travel Institute, 1996)

REI (Recreational Equipment, Inc.), *FYI* series of consumer information pamphlets.

Savage, Peter. *The Safe Travel Book,* rev. ed. (Lexington Books/Macmillan, 1993).

"Traveling on the Soft Side," *Consumer Reports*, May 1994.

Weiland, Barbara, and Leslie Wood. *Clothes Sense: Straight Talking About Wardrobe Planning* (Palmer/Pletsch, 1984).

Whirlpool Laundry Guide, *Automatic Washers* (Whirlpool Corp., 1988).

Wood, Robert S. *Pleasure Packing* (Ten Speed Press, 1992).

Zepatos, Thalia. *A Journey of One's Own: Uncommon Advice for the Independent Woman Traveler* (The Eighth Mountain Press, 1992).

Dear Overpackers:

I hope that *The Packing Book* has been helpful to you. If you have any:

- ▼ travel tips,
- ▼ overpacked luggage "horror" stories,
- ▼ positive carry-on experiences,
- ▼ favorite luggage or gear,
- ▼ clothing ideas and experiences,
- ▼ packing tips,

or simply any feedback or suggestions at all, please write to me:

Judy Gilford
c/o Ten Speed Press
P.O. Box 7123
Berkeley, CA 94707

Your tips may be included in my next book!

Index

Underwear, 79, 205
  packing, 111
Unpacking, 114–115
U.S. Customs, going through, 56, 185, 186–188
U.S. Embassy, 180
Vacation packing, 137–157
Vaccinations, 45, 203
Valuables
  packing, 39–40, 101
  protecting, 180
Value Added Tax (VAT)
  exemptions, 187
Videotapes, protecting, 25
Voltage and Outlet types table, 60–61
Waist belts
  for cameras, 24
  security wallet, 38
Wallets. *See* Security wallets
Wardrobes. *See also* Travel gear
  adventure travel, 148–152
  babies', 165–166
  backpacking, cycling, hosteling, 155–156 beach, resort, cruise, 146–148
  business trip, 127–135
  children's, 165–166
  cold weather, 152–153
  desert travel, 155
  how to choose, 68–77
  how to choose children's, 163
  mountain travel, 152
  teenagers', 175–176
  tropical travel, 153–155
  vacation, 137–143
  vacation to Europe, 143–146
  weekend getaways, 148
Warm to hot weather
  fabrics for, 73
  insulating layer clothing for, 80–83
  and lipstick, 49
  underlayer clothing for, 78–79
  wardrobes, 153–156
Water bottles, 45

Waterproof fabrics, 200
Waterproof pouches, 39, 208
Water purification equipment, 45–46
Water-repellent vs. waterproof garments, 83–84
Wayfarer (Ex Officio), 154
Weather. *See also* Climates
  researching, 92
Weatherproofing luggage, 27
Websites. *See* Resources
Weekend getaway wardrobe, 148
Weight limits for luggage, 6
Wheelaboards. *See* Wheeled luggage
Wheeled luggage, 14, 18, 19, 20
  choosing, 17–20, 27–28, 33
  for kids, 158
  Office on Wheels, 24
  suiter option, 19, 118, 125
  travel packs with wheels, 16, 19
Women
  business travel wardrobes, 128–133
  personal items for, 50
  traveling abroad, 76–77
  traveling alone, 35
Women's Packing List, 93, 97
Wool, 71
  handwashing, 85–86
World Class Passport Carrier (Coconuts), 37–38, 179, 212
Wrinkle Free, 53, 87
Wrinkles in clothes
  avoiding, 85, 103, 109, 110, 114
  removing, 52–53, 86–87
Z-fold method, 114. *See also* Interfolding method
Zippers on luggage, 28